COLERIDGE
The Early Family Letters

COLERIDGE

The Early Family Letters

EDITED WITH AN INTRODUCTION

BY

JAMES ENGELL

CLARENDON PRESS · OXFORD
1994

Oxford University Press, Walton Street, Oxford OX2 6DP
Oxford New York
Athens Auckland Bangkok Bombay
Calcutta Cape Town Dar es Salaam Delhi
Florence Hong Kong Istanbul Karachi
Kuala Lumpur Madras Madrid Melbourne
Mexico City Nairobi Paris Singapore
Taipei Tokyo Toronto
and associated companies in
Berlin Ibadan

Oxford is a trade mark of Oxford University Press

Published in the United States
By Oxford University Press Inc., New York

British Library Cataloguing in Publication Data
Data available

Library of Congress Cataloging in Publication Data
Coleridge, Samuel Taylor, 1772–1834.
Coleridge, the early family letters / edited with an introduction
by James Engell.
Includes index.
1. Coleridge, Samuel Taylor, 1772–1834—Correspondence.
2. Coleridge, Samuel Taylor, 1772–1834—Family.   3. Poets,
English—19th century—Correspondence.   I. Engell, James, 1951–
II. Title.
PR4483.A4 1994
821'.7—dc20   [B]   94-15165
ISBN 0-19-818244-9

1 3 5 7 9 10 8 6 4 2

Typeset by Graphicraft Typesetters Ltd., Hong Kong

Printed in Great Britain
on acid-free paper by
Biddles Ltd.,
Guildford and King's Lynn

Foreword

I AM very glad that my friend Jim Engell has edited and introduced this book relating my forebear Samuel Taylor Coleridge to his immediate family at Ottery St Mary, the place of his birth and formative years, through early family letters. This collection, published 160 years after Coleridge's death, will be a new reminder of the poet's deep affection for his native home and of the intimate, often complex, relationships within the family. The letters well illustrate the nature and strength of the bonds that existed in that generation and paint its history in vivid detail.

Jim Engell is Professor of English and Comparative Literature at Harvard University and has been involved in Coleridge studies for many years. His frank but sympathetic understanding of STC's life is delightful, and the assembly of these early letters is an important key to understanding Coleridge's philosophical works and enjoying a number of his poems.

I wholeheartedly recommend this book to all students of STC, particularly to those who admire his works and would wish to know more of his family background and how experiences in his early years affected his later life and career.

COLERIDGE

Ottery St Mary, Devon
July 1993

Preface and Acknowledgements

THE main task has been to publish early letters of the Coleridge family, providing enough annotation and context to permit individual readers to construct their own biographical interpretations and historical conclusions. But, aside from a bare recitation or reordering of the evident facts contained in these letters, any introduction to them must also present its own interpretation. Men and women of great achievement who have faced and tried to overcome difficulties and shocks in their own circumstances and inner lives—for example, writers such as Samuel Johnson and Virginia Woolf—develop psychological traits that are complex and unusual. These traits are, in a real sense, part of their achievement. The ways in which they work themselves out may or may not appear attractive or admirable. They usually indicate enormous strength and personal struggle. With regard to Samuel Taylor Coleridge and the Coleridge family, the hope here has been to explore their complex traits and relationships, not to read too much into every detail of these letters, but to present every detail, and to suggest how all the details might very plausibly fit together to form a larger picture.

This small book carries large debts. The Introduction is indebted to, and would not have been possible without, the work of Stephen M. Weissman and his psychological portrait of STC, *His Brother's Keeper*. Other Coleridgeans and colleagues provided helpful criticism and comment: W. J. Bate (whose *Coleridge* introduced me to Coleridge's life and work), Heather Jackson, Robin Jackson, David Perkins, and Kevin Van Anglen. Every student of Coleridge turns to the work of Kathleen Coburn, the *Collected Coleridge* edition and the *Notebooks*, and to the fresh rendering of the first half of STC's life by Richard Holmes, *Coleridge: Early Visions*. James Basker, Jonathan Bate, and Gregory Maertz lent support and wise counsel. On first reading these letters in the British Library, I received encouragement and generous advice from a wonderful scholar—and editor of Charles Dickens's letters—Kathleen Tillotson, KC. In preparing this volume I have also kept before me another model of editorial clarity and scholarship, the Hyde Edition of *The Letters of Samuel Johnson*, edited by Bruce Redford.

I wish to express thanks to Roger Evans, Mirjam Foot, and P. R.

Harris at the British Library; to Christopher Date and Janet Wallace at the British Museum; to Hugh Amory, Roger Stoddard, and Richard Wendorf at the Houghton Library of Harvard; and to David Ferris and the staff of special collections in the Elihu Root Room at the Harvard Law School Library.

Local research was vital. To be able to carry it out I am grateful to William J. Palfrey of Ottery St Mary, to W. E. Wright, Church Steward, and to Mrs Tyers at St Mary's Church. M. M. Rowe, County Archivist, and the Devon Record Office in Exeter kindly extended assistance. I thank Reggie Watters of Coleridge Books in Nether Stowey, and particularly the genial historian of Ottery, John Whitham, who generously shared his knowledge of Coleridge, the family history, and their native home.

For preparation of the text my appreciation is extended to Margo McCarty and Emily Orlando. At OUP it was a pleasure to work with Andrew Lockett and Kim Scott Walwyn. The two advisers for OUP provided astute suggestions and improvements. Research for this volume was supported by grants from the Clark Fund of Harvard University; and publication by a grant from the Hyder E. Rollins Fund of the Department of English at Harvard. The work of Rollins himself, particularly on the letters of Keats and the Keats circle, has been another high editorial standard to attempt to follow.

I thank deeply Lord and Lady Coleridge for their encouragement, interest, insight, and advice. This edition would not have been possible without their generosity and good will. I also thank them and the Trustees of the Coleridge Estate for kind permission to publish these letters.

Errors or omissions are the editor's. Whatever may be of worth in this volume stems originally from those named above.

J.E.

Cambridge, Massachusetts

Contents

List of Letters

List of Illustrations

Short Titles and Abbreviations

Bate	WALTER JACKSON BATE, *Coleridge* (New York: Macmillan, 1968).
BL	*Biographia Literaria*, ed. James Engell and W. Jackson Bate, 2 vols. (Princeton and London: Princeton University Press and Routledge & Kegan Paul, 1983).
Chambers	E. K. CHAMBERS, *Samuel Taylor Coleridge: A Biographical Study* (Oxford: Clarendon Press, 1938).
CL	*Collected Letters of Samuel Taylor Coleridge*, ed. E. L. Griggs, 6 vols. (Oxford: Clarendon Press, 1956–71).
CN	*The Notebooks of Samuel Taylor Coleridge*, ed. Kathleen Coburn and Merton Christensen, 5 double vols. (Princeton: Princeton University Press, 1957–).
DNB	*Dictionary of National Biography*
Dodwell and Miles	EDWARD DODWELL and JAMES SAMUEL MILES, *Alphabetical List of the Officers of the Indian Army*, 1760–1834 (1838).
EV	RICHARD HOLMES, *Coleridge: Early Visions* (London: Hodder & Stoughton, 1989).
Friend	*The Friend*, ed. Barbara E. Rooke, 2 vols. (Princeton and London: Princeton University Press and Routledge & Kegan Paul, 1969).
Gillman	JAMES GILLMAN, *The Life of Samuel Taylor Coleridge* (London: William Pickering, 1838).
HBK	STEPHEN M. WEISSMAN, *His Brother's Keeper: A Psychobiography of Samuel Taylor Coleridge* (Madison, Conn.: International Universities Press, 1989).
LAO	ROY PACKER, *Long Ago in Ottery* (Exmouth: ERD Publications, n.d.)
MNH	JOHN A. WHITHAM, *My Native Home: Samuel Taylor Coleridge of Ottery St. Mary, Devon* (Coleridge Bookshop, Ottery St Mary, 1984).
OED	*Oxford English Dictionary*
OSM	JOHN A. WHITHAM, *Ottery St Mary: A Devonshire Town* (Chichester, Sussex: Phillimore, 1984).
PR	*The Register of Baptisms, Marriages & Burials of the Parish of Ottery St. Mary, Devon, 1601–1837* (The Devon and Cornwall Record Society, 1908–29).
PW	*Poetical Works*, ed. E. H. Coleridge (Oxford: Clarendon Press, 1980 [1912]).

SDH	Lord Coleridge (Bernard John Seymour Coleridge, 2nd Baron), *The Story of a Devonshire House* (London: T. Fisher Unwin, 1905).

Also of interest:

Lawrence Hanson, *The Life of S. T. Coleridge: The Early Years* (London: George Allen and Unwin, 1938).

Tom Mayberry, *Coleridge and Wordsworth in the West Country* (Stroud: Alan Sutton, 1992).

Donald Reiman, 'Coleridge and the Art of Equivocation', in *Studies in Romanticism*, 25 (1986), 325–50.

Chronology

1754	John Coleridge, son of Revd John and Ann Bowdon Coleridge, born
1758	William born
1759	James born
1760: 1 June	Edward born
1764: 23 Mar.	George born
1765	Luke Herman born
1767: 10 Mar.	Anne (Nancy) born
1770: 6 Jan.	Francis (Frank) Syndercombe born
1772: 21 Oct.	Samuel Taylor born
1777: autumn	STC ill, tended by Frank
1779: autumn	STC and Frank quarrel (STC later recalls as 4 Oct.) and STC runs away, spending the night by the River Otter in storm and cold
1780: 21 Nov.	William dies
1781: late Sept.–3 Oct.	Revd John takes Frank to enlist him in the navy; last time STC sees Frank
1781: 4 Oct.	Revd John dreams dream of death
1781: 6 Oct.	Revd John dies at home (STC is there and later recalls the date as 4 Oct.)
1782: 28 Mar.	Petition to Christ's Hospital for STC drawn up
1782: 1 May	Petition signed
1787: 7 Apr.?	John, the eldest brother, dies in India, a possible suicide
1790: Dec.	Luke Herman dies at Exeter
1791: 12 Mar.	Anne, the only sister, buried
1791–2: Dec.–Feb.	Frank dies in India, an apparent suicide
1795: 4 Oct.	STC and Sara Fricker marry
1798: 18 Sept. and 4 Oct.	Publishers issue *Lyrical Ballads*
1800: 3 Oct.	William and Dorothy Wordsworth encounter leech-gatherer
1800: 4 Oct.	STC reads *Christabel* to Wordsworth
1802: 4 Oct.	Wordsworth and Mary Hutchinson marry; Coleridge arranges for *Dejection* to be published on this date
1809: Nov.	Ann Bowdon Coleridge dies
1819: 21 July	Molly Newbery, the beloved family nurse, is buried
1834: 25 July	STC dies
1838: 4 Oct.	Sir John Taylor Coleridge reviews the family letters

Genealogical Chart

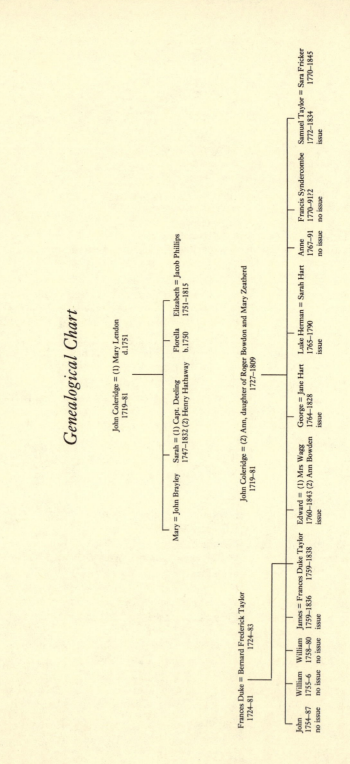

John Coleridge = (1) Mary Lendon
1719–81   d.1751

Mary = John Brayley   Sarah = (1) Capt. Deeling   Florella   Elizabeth = Jacob Phillips
                       1747–1832 (2) Henry Hathaway b.1750   1751–1815

John Coleridge = (2) Ann, daughter of Roger Bowdon and Mary Zeatherd
1719–81   1727–1809

Edward = (1) Mrs Wagg   George = Jane Hart   Luke Herman = Sarah Hart   Anne   Francis Syndercombe   Samuel Taylor = Sara Fricker
1760–1843 (2) Ann Bowden 1764–1828 issue   1765–1790   issue   1767–91   1770–9122   1772–1834   1770–1845
issue   no issue   no issue   issue

Frances Duke = Bernard Frederick Taylor
1724–81   1724–83

John   William   William   James = Frances Duke Taylor
1754–87   1755–6   1758–80   1759–1836   1759–1838
no issue   no issue   no issue   issue

Out of monuments, names, words, proverbs, traditions, private records and evidence, fragments of stories, passages of books and the like, we doe save and recover somewhat from the deluge of time.

Francis Bacon, who owned a lease on The Chanter's House, Ottery St Mary, later home of the Coleridge Family

Things apparently insignificant are recommended to our Notice, not for their own sakes, but for their bearings or influences on things of importance: in other words, when they are insignificant in appearance only.

S. T. Coleridge, on Bacon's observations concerning Histories and Lives

INTRODUCTION

THESE letters represent the single most important direct source of information, other than Samuel Taylor Coleridge's own letters themselves, about his youth and family life, particularly during the crucial years from 1772 until 1793, when he reached the age of 21. The range of these letters increases what we know about STC's family circumstances and relations from his birth until after he entered Jesus College, Cambridge. They explain more fully the formation of his adult character and throw fresh light on patterns of behaviour that he followed throughout his life. There are interesting implications for his poetry and philosophical temperament. Specific poems, at the level of both theme and phrase, are seen to be related to family relationships and to circumstances conveyed by the letters. Chapter 1 of the *Biographia Literaria*, a blend of autobiography and poetry criticism, comes more clearly into focus. In short, it becomes possible to examine and reinterpret Coleridge's life and work from an enlarged, fresh perspective.

The transcript of these letters, while available in the British Library since the mid-1950s, is a source which has not previously been tapped. It appears to have remained there unconsulted. This body of correspondence also provides a fascinating collective portrait of the family from which descended, among others, the first Baron Coleridge, Lord Chief Justice. The letters move one to sympathy and admiration for the family and for STC who, while yet so young, suffered so many losses.

From a broad perspective the highlights are several. The letters and Bernard Lord Coleridge's associated research (see below) reveal that one and possibly a second of Coleridge's brothers committed suicide in India. The letters establish a clearer picture of STC's vital relationship with his immediately older brother Frank (Francis)—which must now be seen as absolutely vital to biographers. This crucial relationship has been explored in one study, Stephen M. Weissman's *His Brother's Keeper* (1989). Weissman makes incisive points and his book deserves a wider reception than it has yet enjoyed (my review appears in *Manchester Guardian Weekly* 142: 10 (11 March 1990); *Washington Post Book World* (6 February 1990), 6). The letters provide context and new information for topics many of which are explored by Weissman: STC's habit of establishing brotherly friendships with slightly older men and then enlarging that circle to include women, invariably sisters, whom he could regard as close friends, lovers, sisters, or wives; family finances; Pantisocracy; STC's enlistment in the army; the importance of his nurse, Molly (the transcript for the first time identifies her as Molly Newbery); STC's mother; the impact that the one and possibly two suicides had on the family, as well as the impact on STC of the death of his father, his sister Nancy, and of yet two more of his brothers who died in England. The letters contain suggestive clues for interpreting not only his early years and biography as a whole, but also his writing, private and published. Specific details more firmly situate his older brothers' concern for him. The causes of his habits, fears, compulsions, and worries become clearer. Repeated traumas and sudden loss, continuing from the age of 6 until 21, shaped his constant sense of impending disaster and his need to be approved and comforted, and established the radical sense of loneliness and loss which he combated through friendships and allayed with narcotics. Family events and conditions cast light on his lifelong sense of anxiety, his proverbial weakness of will, and on the illnesses—real, psychosomatic (a word he coined), and imaginary—that plagued him throughout his life.

While it is noted at the beginning of the transcription that these letters 'would be useful to those studying S. T. C.' (fo. iii), they are of varied and wide-ranging interest. Other subjects are illuminated: the Coleridge family, of course, but also Oxford in the later eighteenth century, and the education of young men and women. Military affairs play a large part in the correspondence, especially army life experienced and conducted in India during the 1770s and 1780s. We receive telling glimpses of George Coleridge's duties and daily schedule as a clergyman and schoolmaster at Hackney. Altogether, the letters reveal the trials and drama of a far-flung, well-educated, but, after the death of Revd John Coleridge, often struggling family, whose careers present a microcosm of social culture and of the affairs of church, state, and the military. We hear first-hand accounts of the Gordon Riots, campaigns and marches near Calcutta and Bombay, and college costs and examinations at Christ Church. One letter presents an inventive, satirical description of George III, another a frank, remarkable account of 'antient successless lawyers like myself', written by a family acquaintance practising in London (his opinion of Devonshire,

home of 'Hottentots, gutters and bears, not to say brutes', is also note-
worthy). The letters underline to what an extraordinary degree friendships and personal connections existed as a vital link in the management
of larger institutions, and how older men looked after or acted as
mentors or patrons for those much—or, in some cases, only a little—
younger. From one point of view, then, aside from any interest in
STC, the letters are intriguing historical documents.

DESCRIPTION

British Library—formerly British Museum—Additional MS 47556
is a transcript of early letters of the Coleridge family. Thirty-eight
letters concerning Revd John Coleridge and his children are numbered (fos. 14–76, letter nos. 34 and 35 are transposed); these follow
a short series of earlier numbered letters and one unnumbered letter
(fos. 1–14). All appear in the autograph hand of Bernard John Seymour
Coleridge, 2nd Baron Coleridge, who speaks in the first person on
fo. 31^b and again on fo. 37 in explanatory notes. At fos. 33–4 correspondence from India House, secured in 1907 by Bernard Lord
Coleridge from Sir Arthur Godley, Permanent Under-Secretary of
State for India, is bound in with the manuscript. This correspondence
pertains to the Indian service and records of John and Francis Coleridge.

In 1905 Bernard Lord Coleridge's *The Story of a Devonshire House*
was published. In that book he included parts of sixteen letters or, in
some instances, nearly the whole letter. He used them selectively,
deleting passages (sometimes silently), combining letters in one in-
stance, and presenting only those portions of the material that fitted
the plan of his book, a history of the whole Coleridge family, one that
devotes only a few, not particularly sympathetic, pages to STC. In his
book he gives little indication of exactly how many letters there actually
are, but in the penultimate paragraph states: 'I have only culled from
well-nigh countless writings such extracts as perchance may interest
an outside mind. I know that I have failed to give a faithful record of
the thirst for knowledge, the continuous high thought, the strong
endeavour, the love of all things pure and noble, the clinging to the
home, on which the characters I have striven to portray were mainly
formed' (*SDH* 317). A century earlier, writing in *The Friend* about
modern biography and Sir Alexander Ball (see below, p. 11)—and
commenting on a passage from Francis Bacon, marked in italics by
STC, '*propounding to themselves a Person to represent*'—STC notes that

Bacon 'evidently confines the Biographer to such facts as are either susceptible of some useful general inference, or tend to illustrate those qualities which distinguished the Subject of them from ordinary men'. But STC goes on to say that for those who recognize 'greatness in the mind', then 'Things apparently insignificant are recommended to our Notice, not for their own sakes, but for their bearings or influences on things of importance: in other words, when they are insignificant in appearance only' (*Friend* ii. 285). His remark applies to these letters.

Bernard Lord Coleridge later transcribed, fully, all the letters he had used for his book, as well as almost twice that number of new letters, and his transcription was deposited in the British Library (the sheets were folioed in 1956). To this transcription is affixed the title he gave it, 'Family Letters of Rev: John Coleridge, John and Francis S. Coleridge and others' (fo. i), and his bookplate (fo. ii).

Besides the fact that *The Story of a Devonshire House* includes only parts of a portion of the letters, Bernard Lord Coleridge then did further research in 1907, the results of which are reflected in the India House correspondence and in his own notes to his full transcription, which incorporate the material he discovered after T. Fisher Unwin published *Story* in 1905. While that book has been considered a standard source, in light of both his full transcription and his own later research it can no longer be regarded as complete. It remains, however, a fascinating account of the family. More than roughly two-thirds of the material in the present edition, including all Bernard Lord Coleridge's later research or notes, has never been previously published or quoted. He did not annotate the extracts that do appear in *Story*.

The transcription was purchased by the Pilgrim Trust at the same time as the famous Notebooks (1951), and inventoried as 'family letters'. The Trust then donated these and other Coleridge materials to the British Museum. File CP. 410 of the Museum details the arrangements of the sale and donation.

There may be several reasons why MS 47556 has not previously been consulted. British Museum (now Library) cataloguing dated it 21 August 1956, a date that requires an extra search in a separately indexed volume, Catalogue 31. Manuscripts before 1951 are indexed in numbered volumes with complete descriptions; those after 1956 in a card catalogue. Biographers and scholars since the mid-1950s have relied for the family background of STC on *Story* or other printed sources and did not consult MS 47556. The cataloguing of the transcription is not under S. T. Coleridge's name, but under various names of his family members in separate entries. The transcript as a whole—as distinct from other Coleridge MSS—looks relatively recent. A quick or less than careful examination would conclude little. The first letters appearing in the bound MS are from dates earlier than the later ones, and do not bear on STC's immediate family.

Kathleen Coburn apparently knew of the letters, and members of the Pilgrim Trust probably did too. She may be responsible for the note: 'These are letters from and to S. T. C.'s father, and brothers John, Frank, and others. Transcribed by Bernard Lord Coleridge. Some of the originals, possibly all, are in the library I believe. These transcripts, not valuable in themselves, would be useful to those studying S. T. C.' (fo. iii). This note is not in Bernard Lord Coleridge's hand. (However, Lord Coleridge, 5th Baron, believes the note may have been written by Alwyn Coleridge, now deceased, a direct descendant of STC through Derwent Coleridge.) Searches in the vast number of uncatalogued family papers at Ottery St Mary have not yet discovered the originals. Kathleen Coburn was already working on the later Notebooks and would have had little if any reason to use the transcribed letters for that project. An annotation in the *Notebooks* (*CN* i. 1494 n.) mentions Francis but mistakes his death and its circumstances by seven years. There is, in fact, no indication that Kathleen Coburn or any member of the Pilgrim Trust actually read the letters, and of those involved in this Trust only Basil Willey actively pursued a biographical study or family history. Willey's biography (1973) does not cite the letters and he appears not to have investigated them. He devotes little space to STC's childhood or youth. E. L. Griggs, editing the *Collected Letters* of STC, does not mention or cite MS 47556, which was folioed the same year (1956) that the first volume of STC's letters appeared in that edition. After more than thirty-five years, then, this is the first citation or presentation of the manuscript.

THE STORY OF THE LETTERS AND STC

On 29 August 1781 the Revd John Coleridge wrote to a family acquaintance outlining plans to enlist his second youngest son, Francis, as a midshipman at Plymouth (No. 11). About a month later, according to plan, the father and son left Ottery St Mary together. This was the last day STC saw either of them alive; he never saw his brother again. Frank signed under Captain Thomas Hicks and boarded the

Gibraltar, the ship that during the next year would take him to India and be the scene of the remarkable chance meeting with his eldest brother John. The Revd John Coleridge returned to Ottery via Exeter, where he stopped the evening of 5 October, dining with the Harts, a family extremely close to the Coleridges. The vicar's son, William Coleridge, had died the previous year, the night before his wedding with Jane Hart was to be celebrated. Sixteen years later, George Coleridge married her; Luke Herman Coleridge married Sara Hart in 1789 but himself died in 1790, the year after their only child was born.

The Revd John related to the Harts an ominous dream he had dreamt the previous night, 4 October. In it, Death appeared to him and 'touched him with his dart'. Though he had arrived at the Harts at nightfall, he now decided to press on to Ottery. There he enjoyed some punch and went to bed, but soon woke with pains, apparently in the stomach or intestine. His wife Ann gave him peppermint water. He seemed to recover, but shortly after she heard a terrible noise in his throat, spoke to him repeatedly and, hearing no reply, cried out. This roused STC—he would always remember his mother's '*shriek*'—and instantly he said, 'Papa is dead'. Unaware of his father's arrival, he had gone to bed early, and of course knew nothing of the dream. What he did know was that his father had experienced several serious illnesses (probably heart attacks or strokes) with the threat of death during the previous few years. The Parish Register records the death of Revd John Coleridge: '*died* suddenly Saturday morning 3 Clock 6th De.' ('De.' for the tenth month; *MNH* 10, 12; *PR* ii. 1056*ᵇ*; *HBK* 11–12; *EV* 21; Weissman and Holmes somewhat mistake the exact dates. *CL* i. 355).

This series of events left STC the last man of the house. All the other brothers had departed, and in the past year, William and his father had both died suddenly. His eldest brother John was in India—he had never seen him and never would—and his immediately older brother Frank would soon join John there. STC would be 9 in two weeks.

Throughout his life, STC—and even Wordsworth—'kept' on 4 October the anniversary of these events in a way that those who suffer severe trauma often do (*HBK* 12, 71, 173, 183). The date and events associated with it haunted STC's life and influenced Wordsworth's as well. STC chose 4 October because he believed it was not only the date his father returned home and died (see *CL* i. 355–6), but also the date, two years earlier in 1779, of his terrible quarrel with Frank during which he lunged at his older brother with a knife and then, afraid of a whipping, ran away to the banks of the Otter, only to be found the next morning, temporarily paralysed from the night's exposure to storm and cold rain. STC came to associate the date of 4 October directly with his father's death as well as with his knife thrust at Frank, and then also with Frank's departure, which was coincident with their father's death. The brothers never saw each other again, and Frank committed suicide ten years afterwards at the age of 21.

Years later, James Gillman briefly succeeded in overcoming 'the aversion' STC 'had to read or write any thing about himself' and obtained 'a few notes, rather than a detailed account' of his early relations with his father and with Frank. The notes begin, 'I forget whether it was in my fifth or sixth year, but I believe the latter [it was], in consequence of some quarrel between me and my brother, in the first week in October, I ran away from fear of being whipped, and passed the whole night, a night of rain and storm, on the bleak side of a hill on the Otter, and was there found at daybreak, without the power of using my limbs, about six yards from the naked bank of the river. In my seventh year [he was actually eight], about the same time, if not the very same time, i.e. Oct. 4th, my most dear, most revered father, died suddenly. O that I might so pass away, if like him I were an Israelite without guile. The image of my father, my revered, kind, learned, simple-hearted father is a religion to me!' (Gillman, 9, 10–11).

STC and Wordsworth kept and relived the traumatic date in several conscious ways. STC married Sara Fricker on 4 October 1795. After one publisher, Joseph Cottle, had issued a few copies of *Lyrical Ballads* on 18 September 1798, another publisher, J. Arch, bought the book and published it on 4 October 1798. Two years later, on 4 October 1800, Coleridge arranged to read to Wordsworth his unfinished *Christabel*. Then, two years later again, on 4 October 1802, Wordsworth married Mary Hutchinson. On that same day, the fateful fourth day of October, Coleridge arranged for the *Morning Post* to publish, for the first time, *Dejection: An Ode*. Wordsworth may well have associated the date, too, with his and Dorothy's encounter with the leech-gatherer on 3 October 1800 (*HBK* 173–7, 184), an encounter that profoundly affected Wordsworth and formed the basis for one of his most famous poems. The profound and lasting significance of the date was not lost on other Coleridge family members. In 1838 Sir John Taylor Coleridge wrote to an ageing woman whom Frank had mentioned in one of his letters home from India: 'Yesterday evening I was reading some sweet letters of my Uncle Frank in his early days in India . . .' (No. 19, n. 14). Sir John dates his own letter 4 October. And in it he identifies explicitly the full name of the family nurse, Molly Newbery, who was so passionately important to the boys, and whose identity has been a mystery to scholars and readers for more than a century (see below, p. 18).

After receiving the news of Frank's suicide, STC wrote, 'Poor Francis! I have shed the tear of natural affection over him.—He was the only one of my family, whom similarity of ages made more peculiarly my brother—he was the hero of all the little tales, that make the remembrance of my earliest days interesting!' (*CL* i. 53). STC turned throughout his life to personal relationships and themes in his writing that would revive Frank's role as brother and hero. One way—only one, but full of resonance—to regard the symbolism of STC's relationship with Frank is to see STC's close and often troubled friendships with Wordsworth (who was the same age as Frank) and Southey as attempts to re-establish that bond. Southey, of course, became STC's brother-in-law. Frank had been manly, dashing, handsome, strong-willed, and outgoing. As children, he and his younger brother STC had been involved in a criss-cross of maternal bonds with both their own mother and Molly Newbery, who was nine years younger than Ann Coleridge. The day in 1781 when the Revd Coleridge took Frank to Plymouth to join the navy, everything about the family relationships would indicate how much STC must have looked forward, as a child of 8 would do, to having his father, Nancy, Molly, and his mother more to himself. Within six months he would have none of them, but would himself be sent away. When Frank had been home, feelings of competition and jealousy had sprung up. STC later describes them in remarkable detail, all in the same letter in which he describes his father's death and Frank's going to sea (*CL* i. 352–6). He notes that Molly nursed Frank, but apparently not himself. There was guilt, too, connected with the well-known incident when STC angrily came at Frank with a knife as a final overreaction to a row: a blow occurred, Frank feigned death and alarmed his brother, then laughed and slapped STC. This incident followed an argument over some nourishment from their mother, a piece of cheese (*CL* i. 352–4).

The account STC wrote out for Gillman is less well known but perhaps more revealing. In it STC emphasizes more strongly the emotional import of these events, and how he believed—a self-fulfilling prophecy?—that they imprinted him for the rest of his life and set the nature of his character: 'from certain jealousies of old Molly, my brother Frank's dotingly fond nurse (and if ever child by beauty and loveliness deserved to be doted on, my brother Francis was that child), and by the infusions of her jealousy into my brother's mind, I was in earliest childhood huffed away from the enjoyments of muscular activity from play, to take refuge at my mother's side, on my little stool, to read my little book, and to listen to the talk of my elders. I was driven from life in motion, to life in thought and sensation' (Gillman, 10).

The theme of a brother rashly killing a brother is found in STC's own and, thus, other accounts of his childhood. It occurred in the autumn of 1779 when the boys were 6 and 9, and ended, of course, with STC running away to the River Otter near Cadhay Bridge, only to be found cold and sick, hours later, by Sir Stafford Northcote, father of Maria, the young girl Frank loved and later wrote to (and wrote home about) from India (No. 14; cf. also *CN* i. 1416). In 1804, before embarking for Malta, STC chose Sir James Northcote to paint his portrait. The artist believed—and it seems probable—that he was related to the Northcotes at Ottery (*DNB*).

We need not explore at length here the poetry and writing of STC as they bear on his relationship with Frank. Weissman and Holmes have singled out some particular works, and Weissman is especially acute in his interpretations. STC wrote *The Wanderings of Cain*, an obviously relevant theme, and *Christabel*, which he read to Wordsworth on 4 October 1800, may be construed as *Christ* and *Abel*, a not atypical example of Coleridgean word-play (*HBK* 250, 285). One early poem, 'Dura Navis', has haunting parallels with Frank's military career. The voyage of the Ancient Mariner symbolically traces the sea route to India and the phosphorescence of the Indian Ocean (*HBK* 12). The plot of *Osorio*, later retitled *Remorse*, concerns the attempted reconciliation of separated brothers (*HBK* 87–8, 274–5); STC wrote lines in 'The Foster Mother's Tale' that envisage Frank's experience in India (*EV* 23). The 'poor mad youth'

> . . . seized a boat,
> And all alone, set sail by silent moonlight
> Up a great river, great as any sea,
> And ne'er was heard of more: but 'tis suppos'd
> He liv'd and died among the savage men.

In his last, moving letter home, Frank had written of himself that 'if he has one fault it is that of being too Partial to the banks of the Ganges' (No. 36). And one resonance to the seventh stanza of *Dejection*, first published on 4 October 1802, might concern Frank's last battle in India, the siege at Seringapatam, where he worked feverishly, was perhaps wounded, and then shot himself. The wind in STC's poem sends out 'a scream | Of agony by torture lengthened out'. As a kind of poet that 'mad lutanist' tells

> of the rushing of an host in rout,
> With groans of trampled men, with smarting wounds—
> At once they groan with pain, and shudder with the cold!

Then, by some transformation, the wind tells another story, this time of a child out 'upon a lonesome wild, | Not far from home, but she hath lost her way'. This image, and the backdrop of storm and rain that permeates the poem, conjure up that night of loss and guilt spent by the River Otter. As Holmes points out, storms and a sense of loss so often for STC point back to that traumatic incident, which began with his attempt to stab Frank, also echoed in 'To an Infant'.

One of the reasons that reading Schiller may have so excited STC was that the German writer deals explicitly with brothers estranged, or in violent relationships, or with the hope of loving reconciliation. On first reading Schiller, STC wrote to Southey, soon to be his own brother-in-law, 'I tremble like an Aspen Leaf' (*CL* i. 93). Admittedly proverbial, this is yet exactly the same phrase Frank had used to describe the chance, fateful meeting he had with his brother John in India (No. 19).

Kubla Khan may even owe something to a letter John sent home from India (No. 3), in which he describes 'Monghyr famous for its wild romantic situation, and especially for its being the mountpelier of the East. About two miles from the garrison there is a Hotwell in which the water continually boils. The Natives esteem it sacred and flock thither from all parts of the Country to receive a holy sprinkling.' The imagery and vocabulary were to be echoed by the fragmentary poem.

James Bowyer at Christ's Hospital repeatedly fumed that STC littered his school compositions with the recurring story of Alexander and Clitus, in which the young conqueror rashly, after a dinner argument, slays with a knife his brother in arms, and then deeply regrets it. STC even mentions this in *Biographia Literaria*, the first chapter of which begins with STC at the age of 21, the age at which Frank committed suicide. Lunging at Frank with a knife haunts the beginning of the *Biographia*. In that chapter STC also mentions and critiques Pope's Homer at some length, the same book Frank had read to STC in 1779, when STC was in bed with a life-threatening fever (see below, p. 18). STC's boyhood reading of *The Arabian Nights* also bears on his relationship with Frank (*HBK* 10–11, 110, 327). The tales from *The Arabian Nights* that particularly gripped STC's imagination when he was 5 were about two men and their competition over two women, mirroring STC's and Frank's relations with their mother and Molly Newbery. STC's father, although he apparently did not speculate about the cause, realized what a profoundly disturbing effect this reading had had on STC and destroyed the book.

Despite plans to execute a number of biographies or lives, including those of Lessing and Spinoza, the longest and most detailed biographical account ever written by STC was of Sir Alexander Ball, published in *The Friend*. STC admired Ball greatly and had worked directly under the older man on Malta. Ball, a younger brother of a Gloucestershire family, had joined the navy voluntarily as a boy, fired by reading *Robinson Crusoe*. STC insists, for various reasons, on giving him the character of 'gentleman'. Now Frank, a younger brother in the family, had joined the navy voluntarily, too. He had read *Robinson Crusoe* well enough to quote it from memory (at the age of 13), in a letter home from India; it is, in fact, the only book Frank mentions (No. 19). While several letters refer to Frank as a young gentleman or in the company of gentlemen (Nos. 15, 21), one in particular, from Captain Solomon Earle (No. 32), informs Ann Coleridge that Frank 'is a very different turn of mind from Jack. He, poor lad, was too generous ever to save anything for Himself, but if I mistake not Frank will always live and act like a Gentleman, without being too extravagant. I was well acquainted with them both.' John had died the year before; Frank would live only three-and-a-half more years. If Ball reminded STC at all of Frank—as it seems he well might have—then STC's voyage to Malta was a voyage of reconciliation and reunion, at least symbolically. It was after his return from Malta that he conceived *The Friend*, in which he writes at length about Ball.

The uneasy, tempestuous, often competitive relationship between the two youngest Coleridge brothers can be glimpsed from Frank's side when he writes to Nancy, their sister, 'Desire my dear little Sam (a propos of little I am exactly five feet 11 inches and a half measured yesterday) to write me, and if his Pride enquires why, I don't think proper to commence a correspondence. Say a great deal in my favour about Duty, business, climate, situation, etc.' (No. 35). The earliest known letter written by STC was composed when he was 10 and sent to his brother John (see No. 12). It was enclosed in his mother's letter but neither has survived. Then, in the summer of 1792, STC visited Ottery and almost certainly read Frank's last surviving letter, sent the previous September (No. 36), a tender and impassioned letter, written in the face of imminent danger. STC now wrote to Frank, but would later realize that his own letter reached India months after Frank had committed suicide. The return gesture of reconciliation was too late.

The early family letters and Bernard Lord Coleridge's research, done after *The Story of a Devonshire House* was published, reveal the circumstances of John's and Frank's deaths. John's probable suicide came after financial reverses, the death of a particularly close friend, Captain Meredith, his own illness (possibly malaria), and growing personal isolation. Frank wrote to his sister Nancy with the news (No. 35). Four years later, Frank killed himself, possibly after having been wounded, but army records secured by Bernard Lord Coleridge indicate that it could not have been after the battle of Seringapatam, as has been thought. STC's account of Frank (*CL* i. 311) gives one version in which 'excessive exertion' rather than a wound brings on the delirium responsible for Frank's suicidal act. STC also says 'his attendant' left Frank 'carelessly'. STC wrote this account while composing *Osorio* (*Remorse*). Frank left an eloquent suicide note (below, p. 97), filed in army records until 1907, when Bernard Lord Coleridge secured it as a result of his general enquiry.

That one and possibly two brothers should kill themselves, both the eldest and the one closest in age to himself, could not help but have an impact on STC. We can now more fully understand why, in 1793, just after his own twenty-first birthday—the age at which Frank shot himself—STC, feeling himself in a state of delirium, openly worried about doing the same thing (*CL* i. 63, 68). His close school friend from Christ's Hospital, Thomas Middleton, left England at this crucial time—also for India. STC found himself lonely and despondent. His solution was to enlist in the army, where he soon volunteered to nurse a sick comrade, much as Frank had once nursed him when he was a sick child. Weissman speculates about the name under which STC enlisted, Silas Tomkyn Comberbache (two variants are reported, Tomkins and Comberbacke), as '*Sigh, alas! To my kin, come back!'* (*HBH* 45 and n.). The early letters remind us that at times Frank and the family used his full name, Francis Syndercombe Coleridge. STC's alias would permit him to remain, in initials, 'S. T. C.' yet to assume a name with echoes of his brother's. Coincidentally, it was to a waiting Mr Tomkins that Frank had handed his last letter home (No. 36), three or four months before he killed himself. STC later claimed that he saw the pseudonym on a tradesman's signboard near Westminster Bridge, but an exhaustive search in numerous directories and trade lists of the time has uncovered no such name.

STC's brother John had once written about 'getting Sam a couple of years hence sent out to me as a Cadet at the India House' (No. 24). *The Story of a Devonshire House* mentions this, but the full transcript of the early letters reveals not only this scheme of John's, but the fact that STC's mother and his brother George had made numerous attempts to place STC's name on the officers' list even while he was at Christ's Hospital. They failed because he was too young, not yet 16 (No. 28). When STC joined the army in 1793, shortly after his twenty-first birthday, he was, in one sense, only succeeding in doing what his eldest brother had imagined for him, and what his mother and well-intentioned brother George had actively sought but with repeated failure! He was also doing what John and Frank had done.

STC probably knew that John had once made even more specific provisions for him as early as 1783, when John worried about STC's education and its expense. General Goddard, on his return from India, was to look after STC, act as mentor or patron, and perhaps be a foster father because the absent John could not. Goddard had known young John Coleridge in India, and there is every reason to believe that the family would have accepted Goddard's help. But Goddard, in poor health, died the day his ship reached Land's End (like William's death on the eve of his wedding, a tragedy striking just prior to promised happiness or security). STC would hear that yet another older man—father, helper, older brother—had died on the verge of securing something stable and promising for him. In fact, the keeping of 4 October as an anniversary of the fight with Frank, his father's death, his and Wordsworth's weddings, and the publication of *Lyrical Ballads* and also of *Dejection* suggests—as does the tale of the Ancient Mariner told to the wedding guest—that for STC promised happiness and achievement were significantly and irretrievably linked to trauma and remorse.

The drama more fully sketched by the letters reminds us that in one stretch of twelve years, 1780–92, STC suffered the loss of six immediate members of his family while he was aged between 8 and 20: William (1780), his father (1781), John (1787), Luke Herman (1790), Nancy (1791), and Frank (1791–2). The five deaths of his brothers and father were all sudden and unexpected; Nancy suffered a long, consumptive illness. The last four deaths took place within the span of four years, the last three within two. While large families frequently experienced death in the eighteenth century, it should be recalled that those who died here were all, with the exception of STC's father, young adults, not infants or children; one or even two were suicides; and all occurred during a critical period in STC's life: from the time when he was beginning to understand the finality of death (for most children at about the age of 7 or 8), to his being sent out of the home to London, literally signed over to be a ward of Christ's Hospital, until he was left on his own—with mixed results—at Jesus College. For the boy of 8, his family suddenly disintegrated and continued to disintegrate further for the next twelve years. He had been close to his father, Frank, Luke, and Nancy. Of the three brothers who survived, he would be close only to George.

Throughout his life STC would suffer from a sense of impending disaster and virtually constant anxiety, as well as hypochondria. As several letters make clear, the family had a constitutional weakness that made them particularly susceptible to illness, apparently related to respiratory infections. STC's brothers William, Luke Herman, and George all remark on this. STC thought his own illnesses related both to his father's weak constitution and to the lasting ill effects of his night by the Otter.

The early letters and the family life surrounding them strongly suggest that the pattern for STC's later relationships with brother-like figures, and with sisters whom the 'brothers' could love as both husbands and brothers, was established early in his life. The repeated pattern of such relationships—occurring at least four times—dominated his emotional life for more than twenty-five years (*HBK* 11, 22, 57, 265–6, 270, 276–81, 327; Bate 97). STC would follow it through a number of times, repeating the quadrangle with Tom Evans, Bob Allen, and the Evans sisters while at Christ's Hospital and Jesus College, next with Southey and the Fricker sisters, then with William and Dorothy Wordsworth (he had known Christopher Wordsworth at Cambridge), then again with William, Dorothy, Mary Hutchinson, and her sister Sara, all of whose initials he wrote with his own repeatedly in his Notebook, and finally with John Morgan and the Brent sisters. STC even imagined a brother–brother, sister–sister pairing with himself, John Morgan—who aided in bringing *Biographia Literaria* to birth—Morgan's wife, and his sister-in-law (the Brent sisters—Coleridge wrote the poem 'To Two Sisters' about them). In one letter, musing on this possibility with humour (*CL* iii. 518), STC incredibly anticipates: 'can you conceive of a nobler sound than Baron Coleridge of Coleridge, in the County of Devon?' He puckishly thinks this might be 'the son of the celebrated S. T. Coleridge' conceived with Charlotte Brent. Little could he guess that his own grandnephew would fulfil the prophecy.

We might speculate that a pattern of a pair of brothers bonded to a pair of women, especially sisters, was first established when he and Frank lived at home with their mother and the dear nurse Molly (who was herself close to Ann Coleridge), all other boys having left. After this, the most direct pattern for STC's brother–brother to sister–sister relationships came from his own brothers William, Luke Herman, and George, and their engagements and marriages to the Hart sisters of Exeter. That web of brother–sister marriage relations (see above, p. 6) became central to the Coleridge family's emotional life and financial security from the time STC was 7 or 8 well into the 1790s. Frank mentions the Harts in highly charged terms, 'the Hart Family thro' every member divides my Soul' (No. 36), in his last letter home.

Again, on a brother–sister basis, STC wrote to Edith Fricker, who would marry Robert Southey, that 'I *had* a Sister—an only Sister. Most tenderly did I love her! Yea, I have woke at midnight, and wept because *she was not* . . . My Sister, like you, was beautiful and accomplished—like you, she was lowly of Heart . . . I know, and *feel*, that I am *your Brother*' (*CL* i. 102; cf. *EV* 85–6). Somehow, the death of Nancy, who had cared for and loved STC, needed to be reversed and a new, similar sister found.

The scheme of Pantisocracy is based on twelve 'brothers' and twelve 'sisters' living amicably both as a family and as sexual partners. Counting three daughters by his first marriage, the Revd John Coleridge had twelve children who lived beyond infancy. The Pantisocrats would not live by the River Otter but on the banks of the Susquehanna; and there would be no jealousy! It is a utopian vision, of course, and a well-known one, but its direct connection to STC's own family drama and pattern has only recently been suggested. There are other subtle connections. For example, it was Robert Allen, his friend at Christ's

Hospital, who introduced STC to Southey; there would be Robert Lovell and Lovell's two sisters. STC had been known as 'Brother Coly' to the Evans sisters; Southey, thinking of Pantisocracy and perhaps STC's marriage to his own future sister-in-law, writes, 'I shall then call Coleridge my brother in the real sense of the word'. Interestingly, Southey's father had died, too, and Southey had once considered suicide. Wordsworth had lost both parents and had once considered suicide, too, with a duelling foil. In all these personal relationships of STC the shadow or mark of Frank persists. For example, when STC escorted 'a party of young ladies' to Ottery he took them to Pixies' Parlour, a sandstone cave south of the town on the east bank of the Otter—and 'discovered' what he had in all probability been looking for, the initials he and his brothers had carved there years before, among them STC and FSC (*PW* 40 n.). One is immediately reminded of the 'name rock' on the road from Dove Cottage to Keswick on which STC's 'brother' and 'sisters' had carved their initials WW, DW, MH, SH, and to which STC obsessively added his own, over and over again, in his Notebook.

A FAMILY PORTRAIT

The family letters suggest that Ann Coleridge was a driving force in the family (as STC's own letters aver), but that the more authentic emotional bond of mother and child was felt, at least for John and Frank, between themselves and Molly Newbery. STC would himself later remark to Tom Poole that not his own mother but Poole's instead 'was the only Being whom I ever *felt* in the relation of Mother' (*CL* ii. 758; cf. iii. 31; *EV* 9–10). The letters enlarge our scant knowledge of Ann Coleridge; they confirm and deepen the conclusions drawn by Weissman and Holmes. Weissman notes that the one surviving letter from STC to his mother 'is striking in its coolness, its formality, and its emphasis upon duty rather than love' (*HBK* 12). STC was, in fact, following an emotional formula long practised in the family. Weissman could not have known it (though he correctly infers the situation), but time and again all the sons close their letters with love to brothers and sisters, and duty to their mother or father. Some of STC's early letters home use this emotional formula, too. When John and Frank write from India, letters to their mother are shorter than to their brothers or sister Nancy. Their language is explicit: they love Molly and Nancy—and John's friend and 'more than brother' Captain Meredith admires Nancy!—but to their mother they give their duty. William at Oxford remarks that his mother fails to write to him. He knows he has her affection, but 'we have now and then a little *Fracas* owing', he says guiltily (but accurately?), 'to my *faux pas*'. She is 'more prone to Pardon than any Person I ever met with', but William states this only to qualify what rests at the heart of the matter: 'she is rather irascible' (No. 7). William achieves a closeness to his father that seems impossible with his mother. John will write home and call her gently the 'old Lady', advising his brother James to hide news about John's bad luck in India (No. 22). George later comments about his mother's predilection for a fine bonnet he could purchase in Exeter, ironic in light of the fact that, much against John's wishes (No. 13), Nancy had a few a years before been forced by family circumstances to move to Exeter and work as a milliner's assistant. However, it should be kept in mind that over a period of eighteen years Ann Bowdon Coleridge bore ten children, one of whom died in infancy and only four of whom survived her. She raised the children and managed family affairs with diligence. When STC was sent to Christ's Hospital it had been twenty-eight years since the birth of his eldest brother John.

There are other connections. Duty of a sort was ingrained in STC, too. The family split between love and duty, persistent and formulaic in the family letters before STC was born, and then well into the 1790s, appears in some of his own letters, and then resurfaces in his own ominous description of the impending marriage to Sara Fricker. He had just written to Mary Evans, whose engagement to another man was now certain, 'To love you Habit has made unalterable . . . — and that I have pained you, forgive me! May God infinitely love you.' Then, five days later (29 December 1794), he writes to Southey about Sara Fricker: 'to marry a woman whom I do *not* love—to degrade her, whom I call my Wife, by making her the Instrument of low Desire— and on the removal of a desultory Appetite, to be perhaps not displeased with her Absence!—Enough! . . . Mark you, Southey!—*I will do my Duty*' (*CL* i. 144–5).

Interestingly, Ann Coleridge, Sara Fricker, and Dorothy Wordsworth were all known and actively characterized for their ability to order and 'manage' affairs. The verb is applied by different people on several occasions, especially to Ann Coleridge and Dorothy Wordsworth.

The woman who was a nurse, family servant, and retainer has been identified by only her first name for more than a century and a half. Molly Newbery, perhaps even more than Ann Coleridge, is central to the emotional life of the family, arguably playing as important a role for STC and his brothers as did their mother. STC admits the jealousy he felt towards Frank over Molly's love and attention. He even writes that Molly nursed (breast-fed) Frank, but not himself, and then, as compensation, claims that his mother 'took more notice of me than of Frank—and Frank hated me, because my mother gave me now and then a bit of cake, when he had none' (*CL* i. 347). But by his other accounts and actions STC never felt close to his mother, especially after she signed him over to Christ's Hospital, which legally could apprentice him and, with no restrictions, act as parent. He began to refer to himself (as Wordsworth also did to himself) as an orphan and later kept considerable distance between himself and his mother. It would not have helped if he knew, as he probably did, that she had apparently induced George to help her secure an officer's commission for him even after he had adjusted to Christ's Hospital.

Throughout his life, STC would feel the need for a nurse or physician, someone to care for and comfort him. Perhaps only his father had ever given him unconditional love of the kind a child needs and craves. Molly had certainly given that kind of love to John and Frank, as their letters movingly attest. STC, jealous of Frank's bond with Molly and desiring it himself, and not receiving such love from his mother (but a petition to Christ's Hospital instead), would later cry out to Southey a great emotional truth, 'But I want a Comforter—' (quoted in *MNH* 36). One might recall Auden, that each of us

> . . . craves what's bred in the bone
> not universal love
> but to be loved alone.

At Christ's Hospital he fell in love for a time with his nurse's daughter, a situation he would make light of in the first chapter of the *Biographia* by showing how Bowyer criticized his compositions by referring to his school nurse (much in the way Bowyer had excised the apparently countless references to Alexander and Clitus; *BL* i. 10). Later, as he regarded Southey as a brother and Southey reciprocated, he also looked for a new mother and addressed Southey's surviving parent as 'our mother' (*CL* i. 99).

STC conflates the figures of nurse and sister in his sister Nancy, for whom all the brothers felt special affection. When STC was ill in 1779

Frank nursed and comforted him, and so did Nancy, so that later he would write, in a poem of 1794, that she listened to his 'puny sorrows', his 'hidden maladies', while he acted 'As a sick Patient in a Nurse's arms' (*PW* 78; see also *EV* 15 and n. and 316, where Holmes discusses how sisters, nursing, and erotic love mingle). The loyal nurse Molly Newbery herself died at the age of 82 in 1819, just shortly after STC had moved in with James Gillman, who, along with his wife, would nurse and minister to STC until he died in 1834. One of STC's last wishes was for members of his family to contribute towards 'a handsome legacy' for his servant and helper Harriet Macklin, a gesture that echoes Frank's gift to Molly Newbery forty-nine years earlier (No. 26), with its accompanying comments on gratitude.

The letters repeatedly bring up the need for a 'second father' to the two youngest brothers. George would largely act the part for STC, as John and Captain Archdeacon would for Frank. STC's lifelong sense of exile, of being torn from his native seat, parallels the language of Frank's letters in places, about being an 'exile' from his native land. STC wrote 'To Rev. George Coleridge' in 1797, and the poem candidly states the depth of sorrow and pain he felt concerning his years at Ottery and later visits there:

> . . . yet at times
> My soul is sad, that I have roamed through life
> Still most a stranger, most with naked heart
> At mine own home and birthplace . . .

And as Frank had speculated about returning, STC even speculated about it as late as 1807. After his marriage had effectively disintegrated, and prompted by his own wife's visit to Ottery (at George's invitation), he told his brother that if it would at all benefit or relieve him, 'I am prepared to strike root in my native place' (*CL* iii. 7; *MNH* 37).

The *Argumentum Baculinum* (No. 9), a reference to school whipping, was a favourite phrase of the Revd John Coleridge, and STC recycles it in *Biographia Literaria*. When STC had run away 'from fear of being whipped' after brandishing a knife at Frank, he recorded years later that a village lady had exclaimed, ' "I hope, you'll whip him, Mrs. Coleridge!" ' (Gillman 10; *CL* i. 354). Neither religion nor philosophy, he says, would ever induce him to forgive that woman. Bowyer was legendary for the whippings he gave, and STC commented on them. At Jesus College, STC was pipped at the post for a school prize, adding to his anxiety and disappointment, by a man later known as 'Flogger Keate' at Eton. It was Southey who while at Westminster had edited *The Flagellant* and written against flogging. For it he was expelled. In all these bits and pieces, it should be recalled that STC made a point of saying that when his brother Frank was not nursing him during his illness, he often beat or physically whipped him, either in games or arguments.

Some of the letters, particularly those from William, anticipate the informal, loose structure of STC's later prose: the phrasing and comic wit, the use of Latin, and the humour employed to cut serious points, all suggest some family traits of composition. In fact, while the Revd John Coleridge's own literary and intellectual publications and pursuits have been well known, it is worth noting what has gone unsaid, that STC's later work covers much the same range: translation of drama, periodical contributions, political tracts, commentary on the Bible, studies of language and grammar. While the youngest son later downplayed his father's efforts (*CL* i. 310), his father's intellectual career and achievements, as well as his conversation, offered a template for the genres of STC's later accomplishments.

Family letters were often preserved with care. It was the custom to read them aloud or pass them around (Frank's letter to Nancy, No. 35, alludes to this practice). STC visited Ottery on several occasions after he enrolled at Christ's Hospital and again while he was at Cambridge. While it cannot be ascertained that he read all these letters, it is highly likely that he did so in a number of instances, and that in yet other cases he knew or heard of their import.

The letters, and an interpretation of them in the light of other documents and research, thus make the life and character of STC more *understandable*, more explicable. They provide an immediate window on to the formative years of his childhood and youth, and the story they tell resonates with the pattern and work of his later life.

STC would proclaim in the *Biographia* that the heaven-descended Delphic command 'Know thyself' should form the basis of all philosophical enquiry. He said elsewhere that Wordsworth had descended on him like this command (*CL* ii. 714). For STC it was, in some ways, both an ironic and a self-conscious proclamation. At the time of crisis and upheaval just before enlisting in the army (the narrative of the *Biographia* begins just a few months after that event), he spoke of the confused 'huddle' of his own 'dim discovered motives'. He could not sort them out. It would be two sympathetic men at two different stages of STC's life, Tom Poole and James Gillman, who succeeded in persuading STC to overcome, if only temporarily, his aversion to autobiographical self-examination—not, surely, of the public kind practised in the *Biographia*, but rather of the kind that searched more deeply and uncovered things long hidden or buried. So, when STC wrote his autobiographical letters to Tom Poole and decades later his autobiographical 'notes' to James Gillman, what figures prominently in both exercises of self-knowledge, painful as they were to STC, are the very events and circumstances related by and related to these early family letters, especially the death of STC's father and the relationships between STC and Frank, and also between them, their mother, and Molly Newbery. Wise about human character, Poole and Gillman recognized that STC's early life held a key and needed to be uncovered so that STC could see and reconcile the trauma and conflict that had been so much a part of his first twenty years. That conflict continued profoundly to influence his personal and emotional life thereafter. It was as if he could not choose but repeat those early events. And STC's monologic discourse in one respect meant he could recapture the first audience that had encouraged him to speak in that manner and had spent hours listening to and admiring him: his father. The image of his father, as STC told Gillman, 'is a religion to me!' And, in a sense, those wonderful discourses remained a form of worship ultimately directed, as STC thought, to a personal God, a loving Father. Perhaps STC's aura of orphaned loneliness, of waif-like childhood yearning inside a man's frame, prompted Anna Laetitia Barbauld in 1797 to end 'To Mr. S. T. Coleridge', her poem warning him not to be trapped 'in the maze of metaphysic lore', with the injunction, 'Now heaven conduct thee with a parent's love!'

These letters, then, are—aside from STC's own correspondence and notes—the primary documents of the first twenty years of his life and establish the family story of those years, a story that in all its complexity and tragedy would continue to shape the patterns of his life and to haunt the themes of his work.

Trying throughout his life to re-create a loving family of strong-willed brothers, and nursing lovers and sisters—and failing with Mary Evans, with Pantisocracy, with Sara Hutchinson, with John Morgan and the Brent sisters, struggling at times with Southey and Wordsworth, and failing, too, to achieve stability and happiness in his own marriage—STC appears even in middle age, in Bate's phrase, as a 'waif-like' figure (Bate, 49). Mental or physical trauma that is unresolved, that is not integrated into everyday behaviour, often leads individuals to exhibit several classic, well-recognized traits. In modern standard medical literature these include waif-like behaviour, a sense of being distracted or dissociated from the present moment, feelings of guilt or remorse—especially if the individual survives while others have perished—and a very pronounced tendency to abuse either drugs or alcohol, or both. Individuals are also noted to keep, often obsessively, anniversary dates that centre around the original trauma. These traits, of course, fit STC (*HBK* 173, 179–81, 252, 326).

The knife thrust at Frank, their jealousies over Molly Newbery, the death of William Coleridge and then of his father, both sudden and the second of which STC virtually witnessed, then the successive deaths of John, possibly a suicide brought on by ill-health and depression, of Luke, Nancy, and Frank, who killed himself before receiving STC's only known letter to him, these and the signing over of STC at the age of 9 to be the ward of a demanding and at times brutal school, these are 'all my woes' that he speaks of in his poem to George, woes still very much present to him in 1797. Aside from his own letters to Poole and his notes to Gillman, it is the family letters that most fully and immediately reveal what family life was like before the tragedies struck, and how life evolved as loss after loss mounted.

These private documents tell extraordinary stories. Many are personal and, to use a word they rightly would have elicited in the later eighteenth century, 'affecting'. The authentic grain of life is here, and the obscure past is realized in the full sense of that word. The letters provide enough detail and context for a sympathetic imagination to rescue and reconstruct the personal histories that make up history at large. These are emotional as well as factual records. They form a sort of short epistolary novel, and remind us how vital and realistic that genre appeared to eighteenth-century readers. They contain vivid expressions of family feeling. Moral care and correct regulation of sentiment appear in every paragraph. Ethical and literary training were obviously of great importance and were actively cultivated (e.g. No. 21).

The ages of family members are particularly striking. Almost all letters written by the brothers come from their teens or twenties—in the case of Frank, his early teens. He joined the navy at the age of 11, became a cadet in India at 12, an officer at 13. Frank's letters convey the dash and force STC admired in his character. Concerning Molly, John, and others, Frank is generous and open. His accounts are often moving, and bear a strong individual stamp. Considering his youth he writes in an extraordinarily mature and engaging manner. We can remind ourselves that the story of these letters is that of very young men and women, and that as the reverses and deaths occurred, the youngest of them all, and perhaps the least well braced to suffer and grieve, was STC.

The letters tell more, in some cases a good deal more, about certain activities—personal and professional—of the family than has previously been known. A few contain completely new activities and events, some of them crucial. A list of activities that the letters either cast new light upon or uncover for the first time includes: how and more precisely through whose offices Frank joined as a midshipman at Plymouth, an act which led to his voyage to India; John's and Frank's service in India; the circumstances of their deaths; the family nurse and retainer Molly Newbery, important because of her closeness to John and his brothers Frank and STC; family finances and the generous aid sent by Frank and John; relations with the Hart family; John's and Frank's friendships in India and the fidelity and courage with which they stuck to those friendships; the close emotional bond between Nancy and her brothers; relations between George, Edward, William, James, Luke, Frank, and John; their concern for each other, and George's, Luke's, Frank's, and John's concern for STC; William's education at Oxford; the military career and advancement of James.

This is a partial list and covers the major points; a number of details could be added to it. The family's fortunes, and the tragedies which struck John and Francis, are given greater detail and complexity. Three words might characterize what is heightened: struggle, stamina, sympathy. John served in India more than sixteen years, Frank almost ten. Their first meeting at Bombay was pure coincidence; after less than two years they were separated, often by hundreds of miles, met again, and were again separated (No. 26). India was brutal. Balanced against hopes of rapid promotion and riches were pestilence, infection, debt, loneliness, and battle. The lists of officers reveal a high mortality from many causes. Both sons generously sent funds back to aid the family, particularly John.

Bishop Copleston (1776–1849), a contemporary of STC and a Devon man himself, 'is said to have divided the human race into three classes,—men, women and Coleridges' (*Encyclopaedia Britannica*, 11th edn., vi. 677*b*). The extraordinary testament of these letters suggests that he invented the third category for good reasons.

Note on the Text and Editorial Practices

BERNARD LORD COLERIDGE transcribed the letters grouped by author, then chronologically within each group. To give a clearer narrative of events and family life, this edition prints all letters in chronological order. The original numbering of the letters in the transcription has been changed to fit the chronological scheme. The Appendix correlates letter numbers of the transcription (British Library, Additional MS 47556) with those of the present edition. Those who consult the transcription may thus immediately locate a particular letter in this edition and vice versa. The letters printed here are reproduced as closely and exactly as convention and typography allow. Some standardization in editorial practice is inevitable.

Datelines, *salutations*, and *closings* are given regularized lineation. In them, abbreviations are expanded and punctuation made consistent. After salutations, a comma or colon may be supplied. Closings appear as a final paragraph.

Addresses and *notes*, if any, are supplied in regularized lineation preceding the body of each letter.

Postscripts or *final notes* by the author of the letter are printed with regularized lineation after the closing.

Punctuation is normalized throughout. At the end of a completed sentence a full stop may replace a comma or a dash. However, if the sense of the letter suggests that the transcription has reproduced original punctuation that conveys a specific effect or interpretation, then that punctuation is retained. Missing full stops are supplied. All sentences begin with capital letters. Apostrophes to indicate possession have been normalized.

Abbreviations and *contractions* common in letters of the time but now rarely printed have been silently expanded: e.g. y^r (your), y^rself (yourself), α (and), αc (etc.). All retained abbreviations and contractions follow modern punctuation.

Spellings and *capitalizations* of individual words are retained.

Cross-references are to letter number, correspondents, and date.

Annotations are numbered by individual letter, not by page.

Superior or *superscript letters* are lowered.

Paragraphing is retained. In the few instances where paragraphing is left in doubt, an editorial decision has been made.

Square brackets appearing in the transcription are retained and noted as such. Otherwise, they indicate an editorial addition.

Notes by Bernard Lord Coleridge are all recorded and followed by [B].

Apparent errors, *slips*, or *deletions* are noted (e.g. 'as' for 'at'). They are few. There are no signs of erasure. The transcription, exceptionally fair, strong, and legible, appears in ink on ruled legal paper of a light blue color. Not one word is illegible.

Angle brackets indicate *spaces* or *blanks* in the transcription. A few letters contain blank spaces of varying lengths (none longer than half a line) for which the original may be damaged or torn out. It is possible, though unlikely, that Bernard for some reason chose to omit a word or words appearing in the original.

Bernard secured information about the military service, deaths, and estates of John and Francis Coleridge. The original correspondence he received from India House he apparently pasted into the transcription himself. This edition reproduces the correspondence and information in the same manner Bernard presents them in the transcription, at junctures that best fit the narrative provided by the letters.

John Coleridge[1] to Revd John Coleridge[2]

1 JANUARY 1771

Address: Rev: John Coleridge at Ottery near Exeter, Devon

Note: 'Jack's letter from India'

Bankypore[3] near Batna, Jan. 1st, 1771

Dear Father,

I wrote you several letters about a year ago but have not had the Pleasure of receiving one from you, which is the only thing that Perplexes me at present as I am always anxious after hearing of your Welfare, but as miscarriages often happen in conveying letters at such a Distance I must console myself with hoping the Best.

The Cadets here are formed into a Corps by themselves termed a Select Picquet[4] of Gentlemen Cadets Commanded by Capt: William Thomson.[5] I joined the same the 1st of May last which has been Canton'd[6] here ever since. By accounts lately received from Calcutta there is a Promotion of 5 Lieut: Fireworkers and 35 Ensigns and I have the good fortune to find my name amongst the Latter, after carrying a Firelock as a Cadet since my arrival at Bankypore.

I am sorry that my good Friend Mr Russell[7] has left this country for great Britain. He always continued to befriend me in a most particular manner for which I certainly owe him the strongest obligations. My

---

[1] Eldest son of Revd John Coleridge and Ann Bowdon Coleridge, Cadet in 1770 and Capt. on 28 Feb. 1781; died at Tillicherry, April 1787. *Post* No. 25, John Coleridge to Anne Coleridge, 2 Oct. 1785 (*SDH* 23–44; *HBK* 4, 21; *EV* 5, 10, 22–3). 'Bowden' is sometimes found for 'Bowdon'.

[2] '*Revd John Coleridge* was student of Sidney Coll: Cam: Ordained Deacon to the Curacy of Maryanoley Sept 24. 1749[;] Ordained Priest Dec 23 1750[;] Licensed to the Lectureship of Molland Jan 5. 1753[;] Instituted to the Vicarage of Ottery S. Mary Dec 27. 1760' [B]. Maryanoley is Mariansleigh, near South Molton in North Devon. The Lectureship meant officiating minister appointed by an absentee incumbent. Molland is near South Molton, and while there Revd Coleridge married Ann Bowdon, his second wife. (For Revd John Coleridge, see Gillman, 1–8, *SDH* 11–20; Chambers, 2–6, 177; *MNH* 1, 8–10, 12–13; *HBK* 1–12; *EV* 3–5; and *CL* i. 303, 310, 355).

[3] South of Hubli, in Karnataka, W. India.

[4] *picquet*: obs. for *picket*, a military group within a picketed palisade.

[5] William Thompson, Cadet 1768 and Capt. on 21 Oct. 1769, a rapid promotion. He resigned on 17 Jan. 1776 (Dodwell and Miles, 254–5).

[6] *canton'd*: quartered, from *canton*, an administrative division or quarter of land.

[7] Russell, untraced.

being appointed an officer was entirely owing to his Intimacy. Mr Palk's[8] nephew who lives about a mile from this Place has behaved always to me with the utmost Civility. His Wife was lately delivered of a fine Boy. They are all very well as[9] present. I should be glad to know whither or not your new house be finished and by whom it is occupied. I suppose my sister Sally is marryed by this time, if so God Bless her and the Children she may have, but I would tell her seriously that I would not be in her Place for an Independency. I should be extremely happy to be informed of my Mother's welfare together with that of all my Brothers and Sisters,[10] to whom I desire to be remembered in the most affectionate manner, with all other Friends.

I imagine by this time my Brother William[11] is a Noted Orator[12] but I hope not a Cheating Lawyer.

You can never write me too often as there are no charges made upon letters in this Country. When you write never committ your Letters to Private Hands, but let them be put in the Company's Pacquet[13] by some of your Friends in London. I beg you will offer my Compliments to Mr Duke[14] and Mrs Heath,[15] to Mr and Mrs Clapt[16] with my old schoolfellow Mr George, also Mrs and Miss Coplestone[17]

---

[8] Palk, untraced. [9] 'as' for 'at'.

[10] Sarah Coleridge (1747–1832), John's half-sister and one of Revd Coleridge's daughters by his first wife Mary Lendon (d. 1751). *Post* No. 10, William Coleridge to Ann Bowdon Coleridge, 31 July 1780.

[11] William Coleridge (1758–80), John's immediately younger brother and second son of Revd Coleridge and his wife Ann. *Post* No. 4, William Coleridge to Revd John Coleridge, *c*.9 Apr. 1775, n. 1.

[12] *Orator*: officer speaking in the name of the university on public occasions. William was 13 at the time this letter was written, and not yet at Oxford; John's reference may be to his brother's precocity.

[13] *Pacquet*: packet boat.

[14] John Duke, born John Heath, son of Staplehill Heath and Ann Duke of Otterton. 'He assumed the name of Duke which he inherited through his mother the Duke estates at Otterton' (*OSM* 91). Heath's Court is now the Chanter's House, the name used as early as medieval times. James Coleridge (1759–1836) married the niece of John Duke, Frances Taylor, who through her mother was also co-heiress of the Duke family (see n. 19 below).

[15] Elizabeth Bartlett Heath (1674–1786), second wife of Staplehill Heath (d. 1759). 'She could remember the landing of Prince William of Orange at Torbay in November 1688, and that he had dined at Ottery St Mary on his journey to London to take the crown from James II' (*OSM* 91).

[16] Probably Robert Clapp, an attorney in Ottery, and his wife. He was from old yeoman stock. His niece, John Clapp's daughter Sarah, lived in his household and married John Kestell (*post* No. 19, n. 14; *LAO* 96–7).

[17] The Coplestone family had given communion plate to Ottery church in 1714. John probably refers to Mrs William Coplestone (*post* No. 3, John Coleridge to William Coleridge, 29 Sept. 1774) and her daughter, but Mrs Coplestone might conceivably be the widow of John Coplestone (d. 1759), 'the last of the family' (*OSM* 97). She later married into the

and Mrs Ven of Pehembry[18] with Mrs and Miss William[19] etc. etc.

I conclude after being pretty copious, Dear Father, your most affectionate and dutiful son,

J Coleridge Ensign

Hawtrey family, connected with Eton College. The Coplestones owned Knightstone, a medieval manor house a mile south of Ottery St Mary. In Sept. 1799 STC and Robert Southey visited the Church of St Mary and Southey suggested that the epitaphs in St Stephen's Chapel written for ancestral relations of the Coplestones, the Shermans, were by the poet William Browne, to whom STC thought his own family might be related.

[18] Payhembury, four miles north of Ottery.

[19] John's slip for Williams. *Post* No. 2, Bernard Frederick Taylor to Miss Duke. The Williams family owned Cadhay, a Tudor mansion a mile north-west of Ottery. Miss Elizabeth Williams married Admiral Thomas Graves of Cornwall. Mrs Peere Williams lived at Cadhay until her death in 1792 (*OSM* 86–9).

Bernard Frederick Taylor[1] to *Miss Duke*[2]

BEFORE APRIL 1771

[bef. April 1771][3]

Dear Sister,

Capt. Graves[4] is a very sensible worthy man and I know of no fault in him save that he may be a little too attentive to money matters. But I dare say his good sense will prevent his becoming remarkable on that head, and I think he and the Lady will be very happy. He is a healthy well-looking man about 45 years of age, worth about fifteen thousand pounds besides his Commission and must inevitably be Admiral if he lives, not but what I think he is very fortunate indeed to acquire such an agreeable Lady as Miss Williams, and with such a fortune. The Coach is made and four long-tailed black horses are bought and they are to be married in the Country in April.[5] But what made me take up the pen is another proposal about the £250 which is that the Captain to accomplish his outset thought I suppose that he could make freer with his brother than with other matters and therefore has requested him to pay some money he lent him, which makes the master to look about amongst his friends for a supply to that effect, rather than sell India Stock at a considerable loss. He will give you on bond the same Interest which Miss Coserat[6] gave, which I think is 4½ pc and as to the master's circumstances I know them to be such that you run no risk, if he was to die: In short if I did not think your money to be as safely placed with him as with anybody God forbid I should mention

---

[1] Bernard Frederick Taylor (1724–83) married Frances Duke (1724–81); their daughter Frances Taylor married James Coleridge. *Ante* No. 1, John Coleridge to Revd John Coleridge, 1 Jan. 1771, n. 14 (*SDH* 62–72).

[2] Probably Sara Duke, sister of Frances Duke and 'sister-in-law' [B] of Bernard Frederick Taylor.

[3] Pencil in another hand.

[4] 'Admiral Graves' brother' [B]. Admiral Thomas Graves (1725?–1802), later Vice-Admiral and Lord Graves, became a friend of the Coleridge family. He had three brothers; all were naval captains (*DNB*). He married Elizabeth Williams, who inherited Cadhay (*OSM* 67, 89). *Post* No. 11, John Coleridge to Unidentified Correspondent, 29 Aug. 1781.

[5] Admiral Thomas Graves and Elizabeth Williams married 22 June 1771 (*OSM* 89).

[6] Possibly related to the family of George Cosserat of Exeter (b. 1770), BA Exeter College 1798; he later joined the army. A James Cosserat of Devon had received his BA from Exeter College 1724–5 (Foster, *Alumni Oxonienses 1715–1886* (Oxford and London: Parker and Company, 1888), i. 301).

it. He will take the money immediately if you chuse, for it is to pay for Jewels, the Coach, horses etc. for Miss Williams and his brother. I was yesterday at the Bank and India House to shew Mrs Williams' Attorney the Captain's property in order for the deeds and settlement.

I am with most affectionate wishes for Sister Ann's[7] recovery, dear Sister, your most obliged and humble servant,

Bernard Fred: Taylor

[7] Ann Duke, maiden aunt of Frances Taylor. Ann and Sara Duke lived at the Priory, where Frances Taylor came to stay and there met James Coleridge (*OSM* 91–2; *SDH* 62–72).

John Coleridge to *William Coleridge*

29 SEPTEMBER 1774

Address: To Mr William Coleridge at Ottery S Mary, near
Exeter Devonshire

Monghyr,[1] September 29, 1774

Dear Brother,

I have embraced with pleasure the first return of the ships of this season to inform you and the rest of my friends of the continuation of my welfare. I left Calcutta about the end of April last, and in a month after arrived here where I have remained ever since. You have no doubt heard of Monghyr famous for its wild romantic situation, and especially for its being the mountpelier of the East.[2] About 2 miles from the garrison there is a Hotwell in which the water continually boils. The Natives esteem it sacred and flock thither from all parts of the Country to receive a holy sprinkling, as they imagine it has the Virtue of cleansing them of their sins. You say my Father complains of my not answering his Letters, by this time I am sure he is convinced to the contrary. You desire that I will send you the Persian characters, in answer to which if you want to learn that language you have only to have recourse to Mr Jones'[3] Persian grammar being much better for your instruction than anything that I can write, being at present entirely ignorant, not only of the Persian but of the Malabar[4] language in both which you hope I have made a great proficiency. We have had a Brigade for some months past up the country with Sujah Powla[5] for whom it has conquered the Rohillas[6] in a pitched battle in April last, since which there[7] has been no insurrection in their country for the attainment of their former possessions. The Brigade at present is at Pattergur Fort,[8] near the Thibet Hills. There is likewise an army of Rohillas about 20 miles from them.

[1] In Bihar, N. India, in mountainous country.
[2] This and the next two sentences contain phrases and descriptions suggestive of STC's *Kubla Khan*, ll. 12–19.
[3] Sir William Jones (1746–94), noted Orientalist and Sanskrit scholar. His *Persian Grammar* (1771) established his reputation during his twenties.
[4] Malayalam, spoken on the Malabar coast in SW. India.
[5] Sujah-ud-Dowla, Nabob of Oudh, an ally of the British.
[6] An Afghan people living in Rohilkhand, N. India, in the 18th c.
[7] 'they' del.   [8] Apparently a temporary fort near Tibet.

By the several ships of the season that have arrived I have not received a single letter.

There has been of late a great reduction in the army, so I don't expect to be a Lieutenant for these some years.[9]

Present my duty to my Father and Mother, my love to my Brothers and Sisters, and I am, dear William, with sincere affection, your affectionate Brother,

John Coleridge

P.S. In the same packet with this goes a letter to my cousin[10] at Southmolton. Present my compliments to Mrs William Coplestone,[11] Clapt, etc. every person who is so good as to enquire after me. In your next, write me all the news you can collect and be sure to write me by every ship that sails from Europe for this place.

[9] The exact date of his lieutenancy is not recorded. *Post* No. 6, John Coleridge to Revd John Coleridge, 25 Feb. 1777. John became Captain on 28 Feb. 1781.

[10] Child of John's and STC's maternal aunt at South Molton, Elizabeth Bowdon, who married Samuel Mudge. Revd Coleridge had been master of Squire's Endowed Latin School at South Molton before coming to Ottery St Mary.

[11] *Ante* No. 1, John Coleridge to Revd John Coleridge, 1 Jan. 1771, n. 17.

William Coleridge[1] to Revd John Coleridge

c.9 APRIL 1775

[circ. April 9, 1775][2]

My dear Father,

I received your very obliding Letter and am very happy to hear that you and the whole Family are in good Health, which I hope God of his infinite Mercy will continue, and doubt not but that at the Receipt of this you'll be happy to hear of my Welfare. The 14 Propositions which you sent me was the same as in our Euclid, which is a Latin one, for we are allowed to use no other in our Lectures.[3] Latin is now very nearly as familiar to me as English, for every thing which is done in Oxford is in Latin, at least in our College, which is by much the strictest in the University. We go twice a Day in Latin Prayers, unless in Passion Week and Saints' Days with their Eves when the English Chapel is made use of.

My Upholster's Bill for my Bed, papering my Room, 3 Chairs is yet unpaid: the painter's Bill due (which will come to about 11 shillings) the Taylor's Bill for my Cap, Gown, and a pair of Breeches, which Dr Rt[4] ordered for me before my Cloaths came my others being in a scandalous condition is yet unpaid.

Scout, Shoe-cleaner has	5s per qr or	£1 per annum
Bedmaker	6s	£1 : 4
College Decrements[5] have	£4·10·0 - -	£19·4.

[1] 'Foster's *Alumni* has the following[:] Coleridge, William, s[on]. John of St Mary Ottery (Devon) Cler: Christchurch matric: 3 June 1774 aged 16, Wadham Coll: BA 1779. Extracts from Rev: R B Gardiner's Registers of Wadham ii 154 William Coleridge 1. Matriculated at Ch: Ch: as servitor 3 June 1774 2. Caution money paid as Commoner of Wadham April 22 1777. (this was repaid 14th May 1782 to his brother George. [)] 3. Admitted Scholar of Wadham 30 Sept 1777[;] took the Scholar's oath 5 May 1778[;] Hody Greek Exhibitioner of Wadham 1778–9 4. Took his BA from Wadham 17 March 1779 5. Took his MA from Pembroke 27 April 1780[.] / William Coleridge was ordained Deacon June 4. 1780 and licensed to the Curacy of Ottery S Mary June 5. 1780' [B]. He died that same year, the first of STC's six immediate family to die during 1780–92, his father, four grown brothers, and his only sister (*SDH* 52–4).

[2] Pencil in another hand.

[3] Texts of Euclid were in English, Latin, Greek, or dual languages. A Latin–Greek Euclid remains in the library at the Chanter's House.

[4] Dr Right? untraced.

[5] *Decrements*: '3. Applied to certain college expenses at Oxford. *Obs.* 1726 R. Newton in *Reminiscences* (Oxf. Hist. Soc.) 64 Decrements, each Scholar's proportion for Fuel, Candles,

unless for the first quarter when 3 shillings more is paid. It is uncertain in Regard to the Buttery Book, whether you battle more or less, or have more or less paid you. I was entered in a very unlucky Time, as some of two Terms less standing will determine Batchelors as soon as I shall, viz. in the Lent Term. Had I been entered but a month before, it would have saved me almost a Year in Regard to determining. I would therefore advise you to send Mr Brooke[6] in a Lent Term. My Room will cost me four Pounds a year, so dear is a *nasty stinking* garret as mine was before I came into it, in our College: and I ought to think myself very happy in having such a one, for many of my Seniors will be forced to quit their Rooms for the Students and perhaps *Lugg* out of College for a long time. When the Members of our College are all together, the Butter told me they were 380, but they are never all together in one Term.

You have in your Letter advised me to take Ward[7] in hand. I did for some time and should have continued, but Mr Jackson[8] the greatest Math: in Oxford and the finest Grecian perhaps in England, very closely insisted that we by no means should mix Algebra with Geometry, which were two as distinct Sciences as possible, and used such plain arguments to the contrary, quoted Sir Issac Newton who says he was much put back in the Beginning of his Learning by the Folly of mixing the two Sciences together, and advises People to be very careful, how they do learn Algebra with Euclid; that Euclid was the way to learn Algebra, and that Algebra would, when they were tolerably good Geometricians, be very useful to them in the Analysis of it. Mr Jackson is Public Lecturer. This I hope my dear Father will allow to be a good excuse for what I have done.

Lent Term is now ended. It is a Custom in this College alone to shew up Collections[9] in the Hall, where we were examined by the Sub. Dean, and the Masters of Arts. Some people will not hesitate to say that we undergo a stricter Exam than for a Batchelor of Arts. We must carry up Greek and Latin Books, abridge or write notes on

Salt, and other common necessaries: originally so call'd as so much did, on these accounts, *descrescere*, or was discounted from a Scholar's Endowment' (*OED*).

[6] Probably a student of Revd Coleridge's at the King's New Grammar School. The extant register of pupils begins in 1795.

[7] John Ward of Chester wrote some twenty mathematical textbooks widely used in the 18th c. William may refer to *The Young Mathematician's Guide* (12 edns., 1707–71).

[8] 'Cyril Jackson, subsequently Dean of Ch: Ch:' [B]. Cyril Jackson (1740–1819) was Dean 1783–1809. British Library lists *Herodotus, the Historian* 'edited by J. Stokes, under the superintendence of Dr. Cyril Jackson'.

[9] Examinations given at the end of each term in Oxford colleges.

them. I have acquired no little Honour by these Collections, for before I had construed two minutes, the Sub. Dean bid me stop, gave me an Encomium on my construing Greek so well. Mr Jackson applauded me. Randolph,[10] the Logician said very few such young men could construe Greek so well: and Mr Pettingal,[11] the Censor, said that a man might know from my College Exercises, if he had not heard me construe, that I was a very accomplished young man. These Praises from some of the greatest Scholars in this University could not fail of creating a Blush in my Face. I went to my Rooms, however, in a very good Humor, quite happy and taken up with the Thoughts of the preceding morning and (if I remember rightly) made a better Dinner that Day, than for a week past.

I have sent you my Bill, or Account, in which I hope you will see nothing unnecessary. A few oranges, or Apples, you would, I think, by no means deny me. I am very sorry that my Uncle's Seal should break. I had it mended at the Watchmakers which cost me 2 shillings—It broke again, and I would lay out no more money about it, so I bought a new one for 4 shillings. The Curiosity which cost me a shilling was seen by almost every Member of the University, Doctors, Procters etc. and was indeed very curious.

I sometimes go not out of College for a Week together, tho: Dr Rt advised me to walk frequently.

As for the Article Predestination I am oblidged to you for the Explanation of it, and I wish I could reconcile myself to it better, but shall rest as happy as possible, relying on a merciful Creator, who will not certainly punish the Man that deserves no Punishment.

I should be glad if you would send a Bill of about £10, if it is convenient for Dr Rt has asked me often whether I have paid off my Bills, as the Tradesmen all bring their Bills to him, that he may know whether I have had anything unnecessary or not. [No closing]

[William Coleridge]

[10] 'John Randolph who in 1782 became Regius Professor of Greek, and then of Divinity, and later Bishop of Oxford[.] His portrait hangs on the walls at Cuddesdon Palace' [B]. Randolph (1749–1813) was also Professor of Poetry at Oxford (1776–83) and finally Bishop of London (1809).

[11] 'John Pettingal, Censor 1774–79, went then to Westminster School, and then to a country living' [B]. Pettingal (1745–1826) became rector of E. Hampstead, Berkshire.

No. 5

Robert Hamilton[1] to *Revd John Coleridge*

20 DECEMBER 1775

London, December 20, 1775

Sir:

I have not been unmindful of my promise to endeavour to get your son[2] a Commission and spoke to the Secretary at War[3] for that purpose on Saturday last. He desired to know his age and whether your ability could extend to the fitting him out properly and making him some little annual allowance in addition to his pay whilst he was an Ensign, that not being deemed sufficient for their maintaining themselves properly.[4] I suppose your son to be now about sixteen (the age prescribed). You will let me know this with his heighth and how far you will be able to assist him. If your answer should correspond with my wishes Lord Barrington will put him upon his list and will no doubt provide for him.

I am, Sir, your very Humble Servant,

Robt Hamilton

[1] Possibly Robert Hamilton (1750–1831), a lawyer and legal writer (*DNB*), who may have been an aide in the War Office; or Robert Hamilton, made Lt. Col. in 73rd Highland Foot in 1778?

[2] James, 16 at the time.

[3] William, 2nd Viscount Barrington (1717–92) was Secretary of War 1765–78.

[4] James left home with ten guineas sewn into his waistcoat (*SDH* 62–72). He enjoyed a long and successful military career.

No. 6

John Coleridge to *Revd John Coleridge*

25 FEBRUARY 1777

Ramgur,[1] February 25, 1777

Dear Father,

I had the happiness to get[2] your favour of the 13th of December 1775. Indeed it gives me a great pleasure to be informed of the recovery of our Family from that severe disorder which you say reigned through all England. The death of my Grandmother gave me no small uneasiness some time ago, however, 'tis what we must all expect from the ordinary course of nature. I am glad to hear of the success of my schoolfellow Captain Drewe,[3] and more so as invited by his gallant behaviour. I hope by this time the rebellious Americans have been totally vanquished by the superior force of His Majesty's Arms, and that matters are amicably compromised for the mutual interest of King and subject.[4]

I imagine by this time you must have received my letter dated about 5 months ago mentioning my being promoted to the Rank of Lieutenant.[5] I must now undeceive you in your opinion that promotion is obtained by interest, one only meeting with Preferment according to the general rise, fixed by invariable rules, upon which some instances of infringement have happened in former times, but in all likelyhood such will never be seen again.

I have the pleasure to inform you that <   > the army will be quicker now than for many years past as a great many of our Officers are appointed to the command of the Troupe of the Nabob of Oude:[6] as I would wish to be one of them I have signified the same to some friends in this Country who I believe are about to apply for me; should I succeed you may depend upon having the most early intimation of

[1] Ramgur: Rangpur, north of Calcutta.   [2] 'receive' del.

[3] Captain Edward Drew, 35th Reg. Foot (*Army List* (1775), 89).

[4] Probably unknown to John, his father later wrote a pamphlet on the American Revolution.

[5] *Ante* No. 3, John Coleridge to William Coleridge, 29 Sept. 1774, n. 9. The letter has not survived.

[6] *Ante* ibid., n. 5. Oudh, one of the United Provinces of Agra and Oudh, Muslim provinces later incorporated by the E. India Co. The Nabob from 1775 to 1797 was Asaf-ud-Dowla.

it being an establishment more lucrative than the Company's[7] within the province, so if everything answers agreeable to expectation, I may soon have the happiness to see you reap the advantage as well as myself.

In Future should you not hear as often from me as you have right to expect, I beg you won't impute it to want of Duty in me but to the casual miscarriages that often attend such long passages.

I now conclude with my sincerest wishes for your health and welfare, my Mother's, sisters'[8] and my tribe of Brothers (to make of your own phrases)[9] with all other friends and relations.

I am, dear Father, Your dutiful and affectionate son,

John Coleridge

[7] E. India Co.   [8] John includes his half-sisters.

[9] The phrase became common in the family. Revd Coleridge may have been applying a Hebrew typology. STC was 'uncertain whether he was the Benjamin or the black sheep' (*EV* 5; Bate, 1).

William Coleridge to Revd John Coleridge

c.1779–1780

[1779–1780][1]

Dear Father,

You will easily conceive the pleasure I felt the moment I saw a Letter superscribed with your own hand. We have Reason to thank God for his great Providence in restoring you once more to my dearest Family.[2] I have paid Giles the Taylor the thirds of my Room, and am preparing a Letter for College to enquire my situation there from the College Books, notwithstanding my Order. This is to me apparently *unaccountable*, but a few weeks will probably clear up the Mist. I have to thank you for your Caution against the cold so generally prevalent, but it seems to be of that Nature, which the strictest Caution[3] and warmest Nurture is unable to prevent. I have however taken your advice by abstaining from all spiritous Liquors, even my own Foible Port Wine, in order that the Blood may suffer no excessive Inflammation, or become feverish by too sudden a Stoppage of Perspiration. But even this and still more extraordinary care has not been attended with the success I had preconceived, nor defended me from an Hoarseness which (however troublesome it may have been gives me at present but little Concern, as the approach of each morning seems gradually to renew my Voice, and to raise my organs of Speech to their *proper* Tone, which is none of the lowest if you will be good enough to enquire at the key hole of Hackney School.[4]

Your observation on Epi[5] and Endymical Disorders is doubtless

---

[1] Pencil in another hand. The letter was probably written at Hackney.

[2] Revd Coleridge suffered several serious illnesses, possibly heart attacks or strokes, in the years before his death in 1781. STC, aged 6 or 7, was well aware of these. He later wrote to Gillman, 'Being the youngest child, I possibly inherited the weakly state of health of my father' (Gillman, 10).

[3] 'Caust' del.

[4] William was briefly a master at Newcome's School in Hackney before returning to Ottery St Mary in 1780 (Chambers, 8). Peter Newcome, his son and his grandson, administered the school throughout the 18th c. It stood on grounds later occupied by the orphan asylum (William Robinson, *History and Antiquities of Hackney* (London: John Bowyer Nichols, 1842), i. 140–1). George served as Assistant Master before returning to Ottery as Master of the King's School in 1794.

[5] 'Epist' del.

just, and such as I had always conceived, 'till misled by Dr Powells Physical Explanatory Dictionary,[6] which if not altogether, at least makes them nearly synonymous,[7] or I misunderstood him. He considers every Disorder which is introduced by the Air to be endemical, but if vague and generally infectious, to be epidemical. But I cannot be *certain*.

I have enquired concerning *poor* Jack, tho' (if alive) he is in all Probability *rich* Jack. The greatest Depredations are apprehended on the Malabar Coast, near which I should suppose him stationed, but no Account can be given of him, or any other Man 'till the arrival of the East India Ships, which are expected in every Day from Ireland. What a lucky thing if he should make a Remittance of two or three thousand in order to keep Ned[8] and the rest a little above Water. He need not trouble his Head then about *Mother Bachelor* and the Coal Bill.

Pray is there any Truth in the Report of a Disorder at Exeter bearing (to the Stygian Current) a number almost adequate to that of the Plague.[9] They are first scared by the Throat strangled and sent packing Post-Haste downwards. I saw it lately in the '*Morning Post*'.

I wish you to persuade my dear Mother to give me a Letter; but let her not wait for a Cover from me. I have none at present, but shall shortly send for some. I'll give her a long Letter by way of Recompence: and more—as she is not fond of Latin—English she shall not have a single Bombast Expression in the whole Letter.[10] You and I are more indifferent about these Matters, and hence, whether I bellow, blow, or breathe am equally well understood, but I would not have you think, that this long tail'd apish Method of Writing is my Fort, or that I am unequal to the Task of writing clearly, comprehensively and (which is a combination of both) with elegance.[11]

---

[6] Powell's Physical Explanatory Dictionary is untraced. STC later used *The Physical Dictionary* by Steven Blanchard (Stephanus Blanckert), which makes a distinction similar to the one William mentions.

[7] William seems to have inferred that his father would de-synonymize the terms, an intellectual–linguistic move later a hallmark of STC.

[8] Edward Coleridge (1760–1843), later Vicar of Buckerell, then at Pembroke College, Oxford, where William received his MA (*SDH* 62). STC considered Edward 'the wit' in the family (*CL* i. 311).

[9] William refers to the 1779 epidemic that struck both STC and George. Sam was isolated with a 'putrid fever' and his brother Frank nursed him and 'stole up in spite of orders to the contrary, and sat by my bedside, and read Pope's Homer to me' (*CL* i. 348). STC first experienced his night terrors during this 1779 illness. Coincidentally, Pope's Homer receives considerable treatment in ch. 1 of *BL*.

[10] If written, the letter has not survived.

[11] The swing from a 'long tail'd' style to one of elegance would later characterize some of STC's work, especially that with personal overtones.

Now I have in my Head just what you have in yours—Well. Bill grows more and more of a Coxcomb every Day. His Vanity is intolerable. And Ned says,[12] I declare, Mamma, he is become a perfect Puff. And my dear Mother—no she will not give her assent, for I know that I am no little share in her Affection: tho' we have now and then a little *Fracas* owing generally to my *faux pas*; but what can we say Vitiis nemo sine nascitur etc.,[13] and I'll say this, if she is rather irascible, she is at the same Time more prone to Pardon than any Person I ever met with.

Betsey[14] is grumbling, I take it for granted; well, as Davus says *Accipe bene lectum convenit numerus*.[15] But *where*, says Betsey, in nubibus?[16] Come, Mrs Betsey lift up your *risible* and not your *irascible* muscles, and depend on it you shall have it shortly. How do they both do? I expected a Letter from Sally.[17]

I now always walk into *Town* and in short *pad* the Hoof everywhere. The Town is a little enlivened by this Anniversary of His Majesty's Accession: so am I, not thro' *over* loyalty, but by means of a Day's agreeable Relaxation on his *Majesty's Account*: a good Husband! his Children grow fat, they say the Nursery is his Room of State, and the largest Room in the Palace; it is his Audience Room, vagitus et ingens, as you may suppose, infantumque aninice[18] etc. in limine primo. God bless that! optimum nutritorem G. III Regem Fidei Domesticce Defensorem.[19]

[No closing]

[William Coleridge]

---

[12] 'saps' del.

[13] Horace, *Satires* 1.3.68, 'No one is born without faults.'

[14] Elizabeth (1751–1815), William's half-sister, who was ill.

[15] Misquoted from Terence, *Phormio*, 1.52–3, where Davos says, '*Accipe, em: lectumst; conveniet numberus quantum debui*', 'Take it, then; no clipped coin, the sum just what I owed.' Revd John Coleridge had translated *Phormio* and sent his version to David Garrick in hopes of stage performance (Gillman, 2–8; Chambers, 4).

[16] *in nubibus*: in the clouds? Betsey is apparently concerned about rent or money owed.

[17] His half-sister Sarah.

[18] A slip for *infantiumque amici*, possibly in the transcription.

[19] 'A great crying, as you may suppose, infants and friends etc. on the first threshold. God bless that! best nurse George III King and Defender of Domestic Faith.' The rest of the letter is missing or torn out.

W. G.[1] to *Bernard Frederick Taylor*

17 APRIL 1780

Monday, 17th April, 1780

Dear Taylor,

I see plainly we shall never meet, unless you will do me the favor of dining with me. Now I have the public office on Thursday next, and if you will dine with me then at 3 o clock exactly, I will sit with you till half an hour after 5, or near 6, at home and then remove to the office and drink tea there; and I will ask Mr Maxwell and Kirkham[2] or not as you like best. What say you? I am at all sixes and sevens and can only give you port and a common dinner, as in the days of our roasted fowl, which were, however in my opinion the happiest of our life, when our spirits were young, expectation on the wing, and our curiosity insatiable. I am grown an old fellow, you are not more youthy; my views are vanished into air, whatever yours are, and as a proof I am fitting up a mansion for my old age in the Temple (a sort of college) among antient successless lawyers like myself, instead of buying a good town house and having a family me,[3] giving and receiving dinners and living in the world whilst I do live. You are about to do what is almost as bad, retiring into Devonshire, amid Hottentots, gutters[4] and bears, not to say brutes. If I live some 5 or 6 years longer, I *must* be a bencher, shall be entitled to commons and companions of my own age and insignificances, have a coffee-house at hand to prose in, and be a sort of master or *senior fellow* within the purlieus of the Temple, and capped by the under officers as I pass. Having failed of every other object, I shall look up at this, which is the privilege of mere longevity. Why should I repine then no heir or slave? And, if you think, as I *will* I am determined, you will be content and easy, tho not rich, nor great. You ought to be more happy than myself for you have had fewer disappointments. I never got anything I ever sought,

---

[1] Possibly William Graves (d. 1801), son and heir of Thomas Graves of Cornwall. A branch of that family were well known to the Taylors and the Coleridges (*ante* No. 2, Bernard Frederick Taylor to Miss Duke, bef. Apr. 1771; John Hutchinson, *Catalogue of Notable Middle Templars* (London: Butterworth and Co., 1902), 105).

[2] Fellow lawyers of W. G.?   [3] For 'family around me' or 'family near me'.

[4] *gutters*: slang for those born or brought up in low circumstances.

I never won aught I ever played for, I never had a legacy in my life, nor ever had anything turn out to my wish. I have seen hundreds with less industry, less knowledge, less natural understanding, fewer connections, and a smaller fortune succeed where I have failed. And yet I will not burn my books, curse my stars, and hang myself;—but strive to live as well as I can by coaxing my temper, stifling envy, and never looking backward.

W. G.

William Coleridge to *Ann Bowdon Coleridge*

24 JUNE 1780

Address: To Mrs Coleridge

Note: I have double in the Franks to make them lie in the letter.[1]

Daggett's Court,[2] London, June 24 (1780?) [1780][3]

My dearest Mother,

Perhaps you may conceive that I have forgotten you, but that can never be whilst I feel so many marks about me of maternal Tenderness: and I may say without the most distant Breach of Truth, that I never change a shirt without recollecting the best of Parents, to whose Trouble I am indebted for it. Pray let the Doctor write me how you all do, whether your leg is better, and if my dear Father still continues to enjoy that happy state of Body and Mind in which I left him.[4] For my own part I can with certainty affirm that my Health has never been so firmly established, since I commenced Oxonian, as now. I dine with my Aunt Short[5] today; for whom I have been obliged to execute a disagreeable office; no less than the correction of her son James, whose ill Behaviour merits it every Day, and whose Insolence to her would be as insufferable as it is without Controul, if he did not expect a visit from me sooner than he could wish. For no other Person has any Weight with him but myself, arising not so much perhaps from any other argument as one neverfailing Remedy the 'Argumentum Baculinum' as my Father would term it.[6] I am sorry she has no more Pleasures in her Children, for they, instead of soothing her past Distress, are but thorns which she has sharpened for her own Unhappiness. In short, they are the very Counterparts of their deceased Father,

---

[1] This seems to refer to payment for the posting of the letter. 'Double' may be a slip for 'doubled', i.e. folded in.

[2] Dagget Court, in Finsbury off Long Alley (James Elmes, *Topographical Dictionary of London* (1851), 161). William, ordained Deacon and licensed Curate in Ottery three weeks before, was temporarily in London.

[3] Pencil in another hand.

[4] Revd Coleridge would die in sixteen months. *Ante* No. 7, William Coleridge to Revd John Coleridge, *c.*1779–80, n. 2.

[5] Ann Bowdon Coleridge's sister, who lived in London.

[6] 'argument from the stick'. STC used his father's pet phrase, *BL* i. 175.

the same moroseness of Temper, the same Cruelty implanted in their very Natures, which I fear no[7] time or education will ever remove. I am sorry to act the executioner in this case, but her earnest Intreaties and the duty I owe her as my Mother's Sister demand my compliance. Sally[8] is very well and as happy as her circumstances will admit:[9] I hope her affairs will turn out to her satisfaction. To-morrow I offici-ate at Stamford-Hill[10] in the morning and at Hackney in the after-noon. All my time has been taken up with Sermons, so much indeed that I could not find an hour to spare for these ten days last past. Folks conceive a Clergyman's Life very easy; but it is ten times more troublesome than they can, or I did beforehand, conceive.[11] Now fancy me holding forth tomorrow at eleven; and dining with some Gentleman or other about two, and holding forth again at four, and attending Catechism at six drinking Tea at seven, and reading Prayers at school at half past eight, supping at ten and in bed at eleven. This morning I received a letter from James, and my Buckles, which will by no means suit my present character. I shall bring them down with me, and my Mother may give her Sentiments thereupon. I will tell you one thing, my dear Mother, which you will be surprised to hear, that I am going to take the Lace off from my best shirt, and am determined never to appear out the least informally or uncanonically. A mistake was made in the Stockings. I have only two pairs of thread stockings, one of them an old shabby pair marked EC,[12] and but two Bands, but they are as many as I want at present. Our Riots[13] seem to have pretty well subsided and I am the more glad, as several Houses in Hackney were marked out for Destruction, by the most rascally mob ever assembled: two of the principal Rioters at Langdale's[14] have been apprehended[15] both Roman Catholics and under the cloak of the *Protestant Religion.* Tho' I say our Riots have subsided, we are not yet without our fears. Strict orders were given yesterday for a double Guard in the Park, and no Persons admitted of whatever Rank or Quality, a great deal more is suspected. I saw Mrs Hart Chamb[erlai]n and Coffin[16]

---

7 'Time' del.   8 William's half-sister Sarah.   9 'permit' del.
10 In Edmonton, then 9 miles north of the city.
11 STC gives his own version of a clergyman's life (*BL* i, ch. 11, 226–30 and nn.).
12 for Edward Coleridge?
13 The anti-Catholic Gordon Riots of 1780 led by Lord George Gordon.
14 Langdale's Distillery, 81 Holborn, owned by a Catholic family.
15 'arrested' del.
16 Coleridge family close friends. William became engaged to Jane Hart of Exeter, but he died on 21 Nov. 1780, the eve of their wedding day (*PR* ii. 1054^b). His brother George

in London, they are on their Road home. I paint the Ottery folks
rejoicing at their late good news from America.[17] What say Powel and
Tucker[18] to it. In 9 weeks time I beg my Father will make an engage-
ment to spend a week or fortnight out. He will not fear to entrust his
School with me, now become probato.[19] Pray do not forget my best
respects to Mrs Heath,[20] and let her know how much I wish her
Health and Happiness. Compliments to all friends, particularly Tucker,
Powell and Mr Parminster.

I am with the most unfeigned regards, Your most dutiful and
loving son,

W Coleridge

Duty to my Father and love to all the rest.

married Jane Hart in 1796. Revd John Coleridge stopped at the Harts' in Exeter the evening
immediately preceding his death on 6 Oct. 1781 (*MNH* 10, 47, 48; see also Introd. pp. 6, 15).

[17] The capture of Charleston, S. Carolina, on 12 May, by Admiral George Clinton, securing ammunition, weapons, and over 4,000 prisoners.
[18] John Tucker married Revd John Coleridge's sister Mary. *Post* No. 11, Revd John
Coleridge to Unidentified Correspondent, 29 Aug. 1781. Powel(l) and Mr Parminster,
mentioned at the end of the paragraph, are Ottery acquaintances.
[19] *SDH* 53, prints 'bene probato'. William refers to his being made Deacon and Curate.
He was thus approved or well tested.
[20] *Ante* No. 1, John Coleridge to Revd John Coleridge, 1 Jan. 1771, n. 15.

William Coleridge *to* Ann Bowdon Coleridge

31 JULY 1780

[Hackney,] July 31, [1780][1]

Dear Mother,

I have had the charge of Hackney upon me ever since I wrote you last during Mr Symonds'[2] absence, and I hope to be relieved this week. I have dru[d]ged like an emmet—and I fear without any great Profit. This Profit, however, I have received, that it has enured me to Ecclesiastical Duty, and I would say something, but you'll accuse me of Vanity, so I'll tell you when I come home. Do not, my dear Mother, think it a disrespect that I have not written you. Heaven knows I scarcely have had half an hour of Relaxation this month past, what I had, I gave up to my Betsy's[3] Admirer—Sweet Soul, how harmonious is his Voice, and I can assure you he is knock'd off to a high degree of Taste. I shall send Ned what School books I have. Mrs Short, Sally,[4] and my Uncle's[5] Family are I hear all well; for see them at present I cannot. My Duty to[6] my dear Father will relieve him from his Duty; and that in a few weeks. May Heaven preserve him for his Family and make me a Father, when he is no more to my dearest

---

[1] Pencil in another hand.

[2] One of the masters at Newcome's School in Hackney. The previous letter may be No. 9.

[3] Not William's half-sister Elizabeth (Betsey), who married Jacob Phillips, but Betsy Bowdon, daughter of William's uncle John Bowdon (below, n. 5). STC later described Betsy as 'an ugly and an artful daughter' (*CL* i. 388).

[4] William's and STC's maternal aunt and half-sister Sarah. *Ante* No. 9, William Coleridge to Ann Bowdon Coleridge, 24 June 1780.

[5] John Bowdon, the uncle with whom STC first stayed in London for a few weeks in spring 1782 and with whom he later dined 'every Saturday' (*CL* i. 2–3). STC later wrote, 'My Uncle was very proud of me, and used to carry me from Coffee-house to Coffee-house, and Tavern to Tavern, where I drank, and talked and disputed, as if I had been a man—. Nothing was more common than for a large party to exclaim in my hearing, that I was *a prodigy* etc etc etc—so that, while I remained at my Uncle's, I was most completely spoilt and pampered, both mind and body.' John Bowdon had no sons and STC notes, 'my poor Uncle . . . was as generous as the air . . . but he was a sot' (*CL* i. 388). John Bowdon owned a tobacco shop in Threadneedle Street.

[6] 'from' del.

Brothers and Sisters.[7] When Mr Symonds returns I'll give you a longer Letter.

I am, my dearest Mother, your dutiful and affectionate son,

Wm Coleridge

[7] The older brother or brother figure becoming 'a Father' or 'second Father' is an ever-present theme in the letters of Francis. STC came to feel that George was like a second father to him. William would die on 21 Nov. 1780 at Hackney; his father the Revd John Coleridge ten months later. For the paternal relationship of George to STC, see *EV* 14.

No. 11

Revd John Coleridge to Unidentified Correspondent

29 AUGUST 1781

Note on back: Letter of my Father about Brother Frank
going to sea.[1]

[Ottery St Mary] Aug. 29, 1781

Sir:

I have received and shall for ever retain this testimonial of your goodness; and had I known that you had so greatly exerted your influence, I should have gladly reposed myself and son under it; and do intend now fully to enjoy it—only that I shall write to Admiral Graves' Lady[2] of this early opportunity which Providence has offered me thro you of serving my son, and procure from her a Letter, if possible, of her future willingness to assist him, if after some years it should be necessary for him to ask her interest.

You have indeed proceeded further with Admiral Gambier[3] than I have with Admiral Graves, whose future endeavours of advancing the lad I only confide in, without any Promise on his part. I should be happy then if this affair could be dormant for a week or two, till I obtain a letter from Mrs Graves, to whom I shall write tomorrow when the Post goes down.[4] After which I will immediately write you, when, if the boy has been entered in Admiral Graves' ship, his name may be transferr'd from that ship to Admiral Gambier's, so that his Time <   > sea service will not be lost, and I will then send him

---

[1] This event was highly significant in STC's early life. See Introd., pp. 5–6. In the space of several days, a month after this letter, STC bid his last goodbye to his immediately older brother Francis (Frank, aged 11), who never returned, and then was present in the house at the moment of his father's death early on Saturday morning 6 Oct. (*PR* ii. 1056ᵇ; *HBK* 12; *EV* 21), though he later recalled the date as 4 Oct.

[2] Most probably Elizabeth Graves, née Williams, wife of Admiral Thomas Graves, both friends of the Coleridges. *Ante* No. 2, Bernard Frederick Taylor to Miss Duke, bef. Apr. 1771. But this could refer to the wife of Admiral Samuel Graves (1713–87), first cousin of Admiral Thomas Graves. He served in N. America and was made Rear Admiral on his return in 1779 (John Charnock, *Biographia Navalis* (London: R. Faulder, 1794–8), vi. 42–5).

[3] James Gambier (1723–89), made Vice-Admiral on his return from N. America in 1780 (Charnock, *Biographia*, vi, 126–43).

[4] Either Admiral Thomas Graves and his wife were then living at Plymouth rather than Cadhay, or the Admiral here is his cousin Samuel Graves (above, n. 2).

directly to Plymouth or go with him,[5] when I know the ship and Captain to whom I am to consign him.[6] If his name is not registered at all, it will be conferring favour to have his name on the Sea-books. There has been nothing more done concerning your Rates, but Mr Tucker[7] who desires his best compliments, moves at the next Sessions for an Alteration of the Rate on the complaint of one Mr Evens, so that the same end will be obtained for you without your further Expense.

I am, Sir, with the <   > Sentiments of your great favours, your most obedient and obliged,

John C

---

[5] Revd Coleridge accompanied his son and died the night of his return to Ottery.

[6] Frank eventually found himself on the *Gibraltar* under Captain Thomas Hicks. *Post* No. 14, Francis Coleridge to Ann Bowdon Coleridge, 1 Aug. 1783. STC reported how his father was pleased 'that he had placed Frank under a religious captain' (*CL* i. 355–6).

[7] John Tucker, who married Revd Coleridge's sister Mary. *Ante* No. 9, William Coleridge to Ann Bowdon Coleridge, 24 June 1780.

John Coleridge to Ann Bowdon Coleridge

1 AUGUST 1783

Camp near Surat,[1] Aug. 1, 1783

My dear Madam,

I hope long ere this you have received my letter by General Goddard[2] since which I have received your latter letter enclosing one from my brother Sam[3] who I hope General Goddard has inquired after. I am extremely sorry to find the affairs of the family in so bad a situation, but I will endeavour to render you (from time to time) such assistance as shall enable you to put matters upon a much more eligible footing, and to begin I enclose you a draft for the sum of £200 on Mr Watherstone,[4] who was when in this part of the world a very intimate acquaintance of mine, and will be able to give James or whosoever may receive the money from him every intelligence concerning me.

I hope, as I can assure you of future remittances, that you will give over all thought of parting with my sister Nancy[5] anywhere out of the Family, as it is entirely contrary to my inclination, and I shall take care to provide in such a manner as to render it totally unnecessary.[6]

I have the pleasure to inform you that little Frank is extremely happy in the situation he is in, and I hope that ere long I shall have

[1] In Gujarat, north of Bombay.

[2] General Thomas Goddard (c.1740?–83) served in India 1759–83. John hoped he would look after and provide for STC. Post No. 13, John Coleridge to James Coleridge, 1 Aug. 1783. But General Goddard, returning to England, had already died when the ship reached Land's End on 7 July 1783 (DNB). STC presumably knew that General Goddard was to have been his patron.

[3] This, now lost, is the first known letter by STC, then 10. He never saw his eldest brother.

[4] Captain Dalhousie Watherstone, Cadet 1770, Lt. 1771, Capt. of Infantry 24 Feb. 1781, resigned Nov. 1782, 'd. before 1803' (V. C. P. Hodson, List of the Officers of the Bengal Army (London: Constable, 1927–47), iv. 399; Dodwell and Miles, 266–7.). He apparently returned to England.

[5] Anne Coleridge (1767–91), only full sister of Revd Coleridge's sons and universally loved. In 1785 STC wrote, 'I suppose my sister Anna's beauty has many admirers' (CL i. 1).

[6] After Revd Coleridge's death, family finances proved so tight that Nancy went to Exeter to work. Post No. 13, John Coleridge to James Coleridge, 1 Aug. 1783.

the satisfaction of writing you of his being an officer,[7] he is writing a small note to you himself.[8]

As I have nothing farther to add at present except my sincere wishes for your health and happiness, I beg you'll present my love to my Brothers and Sister and I am your Dutifull and affectionate son,

John Coleridge

N.B. Frank will not let me peruse his letter, as the lord knows what he has been scribbling. Be so good as to make Nancy write me.

[7] At this time Frank was 13. He became an officer retroactive from 15 Oct. 1782. *Post* No. 16, John Coleridge to Ann Bowdon Coleridge, 28 Oct. 1783.

[8] *Post* No. 14, Francis Coleridge to Ann Bowdon Coleridge, 1 Aug. 1783.

John Coleridge to James Coleridge

Camp near Surat, Aug. 1, 1783

My dear James,

Having just heard of a Packet going to be despatched from Bombay, I thought it would be unpardonable to neglect to[1] fine an opportunity of sending a few lines to you. I have remitted home to my Mother by this opportunity the Sum of two Hundred Pounds,[2] and I shall hereafter make such other remittances from time to time as shall enable you to put matters upon a much better plan than they seem to be at present. I have mentioned slightly to my Mother that 'tis much against my inclinations that my Sister Nancy should be bound to any trade or leave the family upon any account, for you may depend upon it that I will take such steps in providing for her that shall render the scheme of binding her to a trade totally unnecessary. Dear James, let me request that you will (should my sister be now in Exeter) urge everything that lays in your power for her being recalled back to her mother, where she may improve herself in every accomplishment that ought to adorn the fair Sex.[3] By my honour, James, I would rather live all the rest of my days on Bread and Water than see my Sister standing behind a Counter, where she is hourly open to the insults of every conceited Puppy that may chuse to purchase a Yard of Ribbon from her, horrid Idea! chucked under chin, etc. etc. too bad to mention. For God's sake get her back, don't let her go to destruction, as some others has who shall be nameless, but you may guess.[4] Now, James, enough of one thing is as good as a feast.

Pray have you been to see Admiral Goddard;[5] I hope you have, as he was a very good friend of mine, and further he promised to visit

---

[1] Slip for 'too' or 'so'.

[2] *Ante* No. 12, John Coleridge to Ann Bowdon Coleridge, 1 Aug. 1783.

[3] Nancy remained in Exeter.

[4] The reference, now obscure, might be to their half-sister Sarah (Sally), about whom twelve years earlier John had written his father, 'I suppose my sister Sally is marryed by this time, if so God Bless her . . . but I would tell her seriously that I would not be in her Place for an Independency' (No. 1).

[5] Slip for General Goddard. *Ante* No. 12, John Coleridge to Ann Bowdon Coleridge, 1 Aug. 1783.

my Mother, and provide for little Sam, who, poor little fellow I must write to when I have more time. I hope that you'll take care that his education is not neglected in any respect—whatever. Money shall not be wanting, if I can help it. In your next letter you must write me a very particular account of every individual in the Family, that is what Kind of men my Brothers are, and do be very pointed concerning the accomplishments of Nancy, you must tell me how she walks, dances, laughs, sings and converses etc. etc. You know what I mean, don't leave a dimple out of the description.

Little Frank is here with me, he behaves so extremely well that he has gained the love and esteem of every Officer of Rank in the Army, the Commanding officer of the Corps to which he belongs praises him to the Skyes, and says he commands a Division better than most Subalterns[6] in his Corps, he employs his time in improving himself, and I don't doubt but he'll turn out a clever fellow, the young dog is as fond of his Sword as a girl is of a new lover.

I saw one Capt: Biggs[7] aboard the Gibraltar[8] who gave me a most pleasing account of you, and I, true Brother-like, believed every word he said; let me know how you stand in the Regiment you belong too,[9] and how much it would take to purchase a Captain's Commission from a Lieutenancy. If you are not in Ottery at the time you receive this, I wish you would hint the attention that is due from all of us to our Mother to the Brothers that may be about her at the time, for I pray to God that the remainder of her days may pass on smoothly and happily, at least 'tis our duty to prevent anything happening then that may give her the least uneasiness. I must leave off for I could scrawl all day long, make my Duty to my mother and love to the Family, and I remain Your friend and Brother,

John Coleridge

P.S. I should like to have Nancy's Picture in miniature.

[6] A rank just below Captain; more generally, a subordinate officer.
[7] *Post* No. 15, Samuel Biggs to James Coleridge, 10 Aug. 1783. Biggs attained Captain in the Marines on 19 May 1778 (*Army List* (1786), 160).
[8] Not the older ship built 1756, but the captured and renamed Spanish *Fénix* with eighty guns, captained by Thomas Hicks (William Clowes, *The Royal Navy* (London: Sampson, Low, Marston, 1898–9), ii. 449, 563). Frank came to India on this ship.
[9] Slip for 'to'.

Francis Coleridge[1] to *Ann Bowdon Coleridge*

1 AUGUST 1783

[Camp near Surat, August 1, 1783]

Dear Mother,

You must long ago have heard that I have left my good friend Capt: Hicks[2] for to stay with my Brother in India who is just the same to me as a Second Father.[3] I now act as a Volunteer in the Bengal army but I hope before you get this letter I shall be an Officer in the Bengal establishment. I am as happy as a little prince and very well. I also hope all my good Friends in Ottery are well. I also hope that Molly[4] is with you and I desire that you will Remember me to her, remember me to M.N.[5] and all my Brothers and Sisters, and I remain your Dutifull Son,

Francis Coleridge

[1] Francis (Frank) Syndercombe Coleridge (1770–91), immediately older brother of STC. Their tempestuous relationship was deeply important to STC, for whom Frank evoked jealousy, pride, tenderness, anger, and guilt (see Introd., pp. 5–13; *HBK*). 'All my Brothers are remarkably handsome', stated STC, 'but they were as inferior to Francis as I am to them' (*CL* i. 311). *Post* No. 35, Francis Coleridge to Anne Coleridge, 1 Nov. 1788.

[2] Captain Thomas Hicks, commanding officer of the *Gibraltar*.

[3] John as 'a Second Father' begins this phrase and theme throughout Frank's letters. *Ante* No. 10, William Coleridge to Ann Bowdon Coleridge, 31 July 1780, n. 7.

[4] Molly Newbery was nurse to all the sons of Revd Coleridge. She died on 21 July 1819, aged 82 (*PR* ii. 1117ᵇ). Later in life she lived in the Flexton, near St Mary's in Ottery. Passages in Frank's and John's letters show how vital she was, eliciting more emotion and tenderness than their mother. Significantly, the first surviving letter of STC is signed in usual family fashion to his mother, 'your dutiful son', but concludes: 'P.S. Give my kind love to Molly' (*CL* i. 1). Later, STC wrote, 'Molly, who had nursed my brother Francis, and was immoderately fond of him, hated me because my mother took more notice of me than of Frank—and Frank hated me, because my mother gave me now and then a bit of cake, when he had none' (*CL* i. 347).

[5] Maria Northcote, whom Frank hoped to marry (*SDH* 47–8; *EV* 12, 15). She was the daughter of Sir Stafford Northcote, 7th Bt., who had found STC the autumn night in 1779 when he had run away after having attacked Frank (*CL* i. 352–4; *HBK* pp. xvii–xx; *EV* 16–17). The Northcotes then lived at the Warden's House, next to the Vicar's (*MNH* 47). Prior to his Malta trip STC had his portrait done by Sir James Northcote, who believed himself related to the same Northcote family (*DNB*).

Captain Samuel Biggs to James Coleridge

10 AUGUST 1783

Plymouth, 10th August, 1783

Dear Sir:

A few years since I had the pleasure of being acquainted with you at Wolverhampton where I was recruiting for the Marine Service, since that I have been to the East Indies and returned lately. A brother of yours[1] went out in the Ship I was in under the care of Capt. Hicks.[2] On our arrival at Bombay we fortunately met with your elder Brother[3] who was supposed to be at Bengal.[4] We took the young gentleman out of the Gibraltar and obtained a Commission for him in the Company's service.

Capt: Coleridge favored me with his company to dinner. I was very happy to tell him I knew you, and more so to speak of you as you deserve. He expressed an ardent desire to serve you and told me his circumstances would very well allow him to remit you five hundred pounds. I begged his excuse for observing to him that if he would extend his benevolence to twice that sum, it would be of such essential service as to enable you to purchase a company.[5] He very generously assured me he would send you Bills to that amount either by the Neptune,[6] or Royal Admiral Indiamen. When I came home with the Dispatches I saw those Ships at St Helena[7] in April last, so that they may be expected every day.

I remain, Sir, Your very obedient servant,

Sam: Biggs

[1] Francis (Frank).
[2] *Ante* No. 13, John Coleridge to James Coleridge, 1 Aug. 1783, n. 8.
[3] John.
[4] The march was delayed. *Post* No. 16, John Coleridge to Ann Bowdon Coleridge, 28 Oct. 1783.
[5] The sum was enormous for the financially strained family, and would have been so even if Revd Coleridge had still been alive. *Post* Nos. 22–4.
[6] A ship of 74 guns.
[7] Administrative centre of the colony including Ascension in the S. Atlantic, and later (1815–21) site of Napoleon's exile.

No. 16

John Coleridge to *Ann Bowdon Coleridge*

28 OCTOBER 1783

Camp near Surat, Oct 28, 1783

My dear Mother,

I have the extreme pleasure of informing you that my Brother
Francis is most elegantly provided for. He is appointed to the Service
and to take Rank as an Ensign of Infantry from the 15th of October
1782, so the youngster has been an officer above a year and I think if
no crosses happen that in a couple of years more he'll be a Lieutenant.[1] In future you must direct your letters for me to Bengall, as the
Detachment I am with marches for that Country in three days from
this Date. In case of your not having received my letter enclosing a
Bill for £200 I send you a Duplicate of it.[2] I have the satisfaction of
informing you that little Frank is in fine Health and from all appearances will do very well in this Country. He desires his Duty to you
and love to his relations and friends. As we are all in a hurry and
confusion concerning the March I hope you'll excuse the shortness of
this letter, and believe me, my Dearest Mother, that you have not a
more Dutifull son than,

John Coleridge

N.B. Make my love to all the Family.

Oh! I had like to have forgot. Pray when will my much loved Nancy
favour me with a Line.

[1] Frank became Lt. seven years later, on 5 June 1790.
[2] *Ante* No. 12, John Coleridge to Ann Bowdon Coleridge, 1 Aug. 1783.

No. 17

Captain Samuel Biggs[1] to James Coleridge

6 MARCH 1784

Address: Lieut and Adjt[2] Jas Coleridge, Ottery Devonshire

Grove, near Plymouth, March 6, 1784

Dear Sir:

I lately had the favor of your letter just as I was quitting Glostershire. I shall be most happy to give you every Satisfaction in my power relating to your Brothers. Your eldest has a Command in the Seapoys.[3] I understood the pay was about £1200 per: an: with many emoluments (unknown to European army) when they take the Field. Your youngest Brother[4] was a Cadet in the same Corps. It will give me very great satisfaction to know you have received letters completing the generous intention of your Brother. The Ships he meant to write by was either the Neptune Capt: Scott,[5] or the Royal Admiral, Capt: Uddart.[6] When I returned from Madras to Bombay your Brother was gone upon an expedition. There are six sail of the line intended for the East Indies. I think it most probable Capt: Coleridge will be in Calcutta in the province of Bengal.

I shall be happy to hear, Sir, you have every advantage I wish you. I remain, dear Sir, with sincerest respect, your very obedient Servant,

Sam: Biggs

[1] *Ante* No. 13, John Coleridge to James Coleridge, 1 Aug. 1783; No. 15, Capt. Samuel Biggs to James Coleridge, 10 Aug. 1783.

[2] Adjutant, a staff officer assisting the commanding officer, usually with administrative affairs.

[3] Sepoys were native Indian soldiers under British command.

[4] Biggs means Francis, not STC.

[5] Probably either Alexander Scott, Capt. in 1776, or William Scott, Capt. in 1781 (*Commissioned Sea Officers of the Royal Navy 1660–1805* (n.d.), iii. 816, 820).

[6] Untraced.

Luke Herman Coleridge[1] to *Ann Bowdon Coleridge*

18 OCTOBER 1784

London, Oct. 18, 1784

Dearest Mother,

A moment from business, with pleasure I seize it to perform the Wish of my Parent. I have entered at the London Hospital, there are many superior advantages. The Terms are 30 guineas, about 18 more will discharge my other Physical Studies. I have settled, though very inconvenient, to live with my Aunt.[2] It is a mile from the Hospital, a morning's Walk. George in conjunction with me have fixed on all things I am to pay my Aunt.

My situation in Town begins to wear a much more pleasing aspect, but not owing to the Town itself, no, that wears its usual aspect, but the Company and Conversation of Men of Eminence in my own Profession, the Pleasure of the Publick Disputes, which we hold every week, makes my Station, for I wish to call it so, peculiarly pleasing. It wants but the absence of a trifling Drawback, to make it a situation of perfect Happiness. But to expect it is the Height of Folly. I am Happier now than any future Period of Life will be able to make me.

My aunt wishes to see you. I flatter her with the Hopes of your once more launching into Life, visiting the gay Metropolis and carrying Pleasure to your Friends <   > my Uncle[3] <   > in best

---

[1] Luke Herman (1765–90), seventh son of Revd John Coleridge. Deciding to become a physician, he entered London Hospital in mid–late 1784 and trained under Sir William Blizard. He left in 1787, married Sara(h) Hart, sister of his deceased brother William's ex-fiancée Jane Hart (whom George married in 1796) and died at Thorverton. His son William Hart Coleridge (1789–1849) became first bishop of Barbados in 1824. Because of Luke, STC, then at Christ's Hospital, 'became wild to be apprenticed to a surgeon' and every Saturday attended and helped Luke at the hospital. There another student, Richard Saumarez, younger brother of Admiral de Saumarez, later recalled the 'extraordinary, enthusiastic, blue-coat boy' acting every way the medical student (*DNB*; Gillman, 22–3). Richard Saumarez (1764–1835), surgeon, honorary governor of Magdalen Hospital, Streatham, wrote physiological works later praised by STC for their philosophical insight, and they met again in 1812 (*DNB*; *BL* i. 162–3 and nn.). STC spells his name Saumerez.

The relationship between William, George, Luke, and the Hart sisters Sara and Jane provided a pattern of brother–brother to sister–sister marriages and friendships crucial to STC throughout his life. See Introd., pp. 6, 15.

[2] Aunt Betsey Short, Luke's maternal aunt.

[3] Not Mr Short, who remains shadowy, but apparently Betsey Short's and Ann Coleridge's brother, John Bowdon.

1. The River Otter from Cadhay Bridge

2. The Old Font, used in 1700s: the Church of St Mary.
Photo courtesy of John Whitham

3. Entrance to Pixies' Parlour

b. 1772 S.T. COLERIDGE. d. 1834

He prayeth best who loveth best
All things both great and small;
For the dear God who loveth us,
He made and loveth all.

4. Memorial to STC (Gilbert Coleridge, 1931); outer churchyard wall, the Church of St Mary; also Jesus College and Christ's Hospital

affections. You will present my best Compliments to all Friends. I must write Mr Vaughn[4] according to the rules of Politeness, but I have scarcely a moment to spare. Studies of various kinds fill up the Day and the Night is but the time for recruiting the Exhausted Spirits. I write Mr Smerdon[5] by this or the next Post. Excuse all.

Your affectionate son,

L H Coleridge

P.S. I have found out the lodging of Capt: Hicks,[6] shall wait on him, with thanks of the Family. Inform Mr Vaughn I mean to return my thanks for their civilities by letter on the very first opportunity.

To all Friends remember me.

[4] STC had seen a Mr Vaughan pass over the bridge at about a furlong's distance the night he ran away to the River Otter (*CL* i. 353–4).

[5] Fulwood Smerdon MA (1754–94), BA Trinity College 1776, succeeded Revd John Coleridge as Vicar at Ottery St Mary, but did not also head the King's School. He countersigned the petition to send STC to Christ's Hospital. On his death STC wrote his elegiac 'Lines on a Friend Who Died of a Frenzy Fever', which are sharp in self-criticism of STC's own gifts, 'Sloth-jaundiced all!'.

[6] Captain Thomas Hicks. *Ante* No. 14, Francis Coleridge to Ann Bowdon Coleridge, 1 Aug. 1783.

Francis Coleridge to Anne Coleridge

25 OCTOBER 1784

Cawnpore,[2] Oct. 25, 1784

Dear Nancy,

You are very right. I have neglected my absent Friends but do not think I have forgot them, and indeed it would be ungrateful in me, if I did not write them.

You may be sure Nancy I thank providence for bringing about that meeting[3] which has been the cause of all my good Fortune and happiness which I now in fulness enjoy. It was an affectionate meeting and I will inform you of the particulars; there was in our ship one Capt: Mordaunt[4] who had been in India before, when we came to Bombay, finding a number of his Friends there he went often ashore; the day before the Fleet sailed, he desired one Capt: Welsh[5] to go aboard with him, who was an intimate Friend of your brother. I will, said W, and will write a note to Coleridge to go with us. Upon this Capt: Mordaunt recollecting me, said, there was a young midshipman, a favourite of Capt: Hicks[6] of that name aboard. Upon that they agreed to inform my brother of it, which they did soon after, and all three came on board. I was then in the lower deck, and though you won't believe it, I was sitting upon a Gun and thinking of my Brother, that is, whether I should ever see or hear anything of him, when seeing a Lieutenant, who had been sent to inform me of my Brother's[7]

---

[1] The transcription (fo. 36) notes '(part published B.L. Vol. II. 317.)' [B]. This refers to the 1847 *Biographia Literaria*, ed. H. N. Coleridge and Sara Coleridge. They, not STC, included the letter in a 'Biographical Supplement'.

[2] Now Kanpur, a city on the Ganges in south-central Uttar Pradesh.

[3] This chance meeting with his eldest brother John led to his leaving the navy and remaining in India. The meeting happened months before 1 Aug. 1783; by that date John and Frank are writing home, assuming news of the meeting had already arrived (Nos. 12–14); in Aug. 1783, Captain Biggs is 'returned lately' to England, having witnessed the meeting, presumably some months before. *Ante* No. 15, Capt. Samuel Biggs to James Coleridge, 10 Aug. 1783.

[4] Captain Henry Mordaunt, 7th Reg. Native Infantry, Bengal (*India Register* (2nd. edn., 1819), 52), made Capt. On 25 Mar. 1781, and died at Benares on 8 Feb. 1791 (Dodwell and Miles, 176–7).

[5] Capt. Thomas Welsh, made Capt. 18 Jan. 1781, later Colonel, and retired in 1800 (Dodwell and Miles, 268–9).

[6] Captain Thomas Hicks.   [7] John.

being on board, I got up off the Gun; but instead of telling me about my Brother, he told me that Capt: Hicks was very angry with me, and wanted to see me. Capt: Hicks had always been a Father to me, and loves me as if I had been his own child. I therefore went up shaking like an aspin leaf[8] to the Lieutenant's apartments, when a Gentleman took hold of my hand. I did not mind him at first, but looked round for the Captain, but, the Gentleman still holding my hand, I looked in his face, and what was my surprise when I saw him too full to speak, and eyes full of tears; whether crying is catching I know not, but I begun a crying too, though I did not know the reason till he caught me in his arms and told me he was my Brother and then I found it was paying nature her tribute, for I believe I never cry'd so much in my life. There is a saying in Robinson Crusoe I remember very well viz. Sudden joy like grief confounds at first.[9] We directly went ashore, having got my discharge, and having took a most affectionate leave of Capt: Hicks I left the ship for good and all.

My situation in the army is that I am one of the oldest Ensigns and before you get this must in all probability be a Lieutenant;[10] how many changes there has been in my life and what lucky ones they have been, and how young I am still; I must be 7 years older before I can properly stile myself a man,[11] and what a number of Officers do I command, who are old enough to be Father already.

Nothing gives me such pleasure as to think Molly[12] still continues with my Mother. If God ever puts it in my power I will return some of the numberless favours she has done so often for me when I was at home.

Tell Maria[13] not to marry this sometime, for I am much more likely to make ten thousand pounds in India than one on board a ship, so I shall not despair, but still continue her constant lover, for without ten

---

[8] STC uses the same image, 'I tremble like an Aspen Leaf', to Southey on first reading Schiller (*CL* i. 93). Aspen leaves are known proverbially for trembling in the slightest breeze.

[9] 'For sudden Joys, like Griefs, confound at first.' *Life and Adventures of Robinson Crusoe*, 'I Go on Board in an Evil Hour' (Shakespeare Head edn. of Defoe (1927), i. 52). *Robinson Crusoe* was a boyhood favourite of Frank's and STC's, and also of Sir Alexander Ball's (see Introd., p. 11).

[10] Frank was not made Lt. until 5 June 1790, six years later.

[11] He was 14 at this time.

[12] 'Molly Newbery' [B]. *Ante* No. 14, Francis Coleridge to Ann Bowdon Coleridge, 1 Aug. 1783.

[13] Maria Northcote. *Ante* No. 14, Francis Coleridge to Ann Bowdon Coleridge, 1 Aug. 1783. Frank may be only half-joking about the marriage bargain (*SDH* 47–8).

thousand pound I was not to expect her hand, that was the bargain; so you see I am to marry her, and she marries my ten thousand pound, but you may inform her that I should be very happy if she would adorn herself a little, and that if I should be the handsomer for ten thousand pound, she must who has already such a pretty face, look elegantly with five thousand in her pocket. So you see I am very modest but we must not forget Miss Sarah Kessell,[14] pray give my compliments to her, for I am not in love with her, though I do not know where[15] it would not be a good thing to have two strings to my bow, for I believe Maria will soon break. As I am now in a merry state, I will conclude with giving my love to Molly and my Duty to Dear Mother and I remain in good health.

Your affectionate Brother,

Francis Sindercom[16] Coleridge
3rd Brigade

My Brother is in 1st Brigade.

[14] Sarah Kessell is Sarah Kestell, daughter of John and Sarah Kestell, baptized 24 Jan. 1771 (*PR* i. 526; see *ante* No. 1, n. 16). STC pokes fun at 'Kesell', to whom in 1792 he gave a letter for Frank that reached India after Frank's death (*CL* i. 41). This is the same as Frank's 'Kessell'. STC is sceptical 'of the most wonderful prospects' entertained by his mother for Frank. Ann Coleridge thought the Kestells well connected. STC disliked John Kestell, 'very much part of the high society' of Ottery and a 'doctor of Tory politics'. His daughter married George Cornish, who became aide-de-camp to his brother-in-law Sir John Shore, later Governor General of India and made Lord Teignmouth. He returned from India to live at Salcombe Regis (*LAO* 96–7). STC may also have harboured mixed feelings about John Kestell because he had signed Ann Coleridge's petition to send STC to Christ's Hospital in 1782.

'In a letter to this lady then Mrs Cornish[,] Salcombe Hill, Sidmouth dated Oct. 4, 1838[,] My grandfather Sir John Taylor Coleridge says "Yesterday evening I was reading some sweet letters of my Uncle Frank in his early days in India in one of which he speaks of you and Maria Northcote as 'two strings to his bow' I must say, however, to the shame of his gallantry, but not of his heart, that it seems to run over more with tenderness towards poor Molly Newbery than towards either of you young belles" ' [B]. Sir John Taylor Coleridge (1790–1876), the noted Judge, son of James and father of John Duke Coleridge, 1st Baron (1820–94) and Lord Chief Justice of the Queen's Bench (1880–94), was re-reading Frank's letters and writing to Mrs Cornish, John Kestell's daughter (b. 1770) on the exact anniversary date, 4 Oct., of the day Revd John Coleridge had his dream of Death, an anniversary obsessively 'kept' by STC and associated by STC with his quarrel with Frank and, later, Frank's departure from Ottery and England (Introd., pp. 5–8).

[15] For 'whether' or 'that'.

[16] The family usually spelled Frank's middle name Syndercombe.

Francis Coleridge to Ann Bowdon Coleridge

10 NOVEMBER 1784

Camp at Lucknow,[1] Nov. 10, 1784

My dear and Honoured Mother,

My Brother[2] will have acquainted you more than once with his situations and my own since the period of my quitting the Gibraltar:[3] a short time before we left Surat I gave him a letter to be forwarded with his own, and such as it was, I hope you have received it.[4] In future my Dear and only Parent you shall hear regularly and punctually immediately from myself.

Upon the arrival of our Detachment near Bengall, it was broke, and the Batallions that composed it sent to the different Brigades. The supernumerary Officers of all Ranks were ordered to join the European Regiments; this order affected my Brother and me. But through the Interest of my Friends and that good luck which has attended me in general, I was so Fortunate as to get reappointed to my former station in the 6th Regiment of Bengall Sepoys, or Soldiers in which Corps my Brother served thirteen years.

We are now separated, he to the 2nd Brigade, and I with the 3rd which is now in the Field, however providence has provided me with a Friend[5] with whom I live as I did with him. My Brother's behaviour towards me has at all times been truly affectionate, indeed so much so that my Faults were seldom corrected, nor did I see him in any other light than that of a Fond and indulgent Friend, ready to gratify all my little whims and caprices. However he was not so blind to my Interest, but he saw the advantages of a separation, and yet parted from me with great reluctance, tho' he knew I could not be taken better care of by any Person than by the Gentleman in whose charge he left me.

Captain Archdeacon[6] with whom I live has promised to assist me

---

[1] In Uttar Pradesh, about 40 miles north-east of the Ganges.

[2] John.

[3] The ship on which Frank arrived in India. *Ante* No. 15, Capt. Samuel Biggs to James Coleridge, 10 Aug. 1783.

[4] No. 14, Francis Coleridge to Ann Bowdon Coleridge, 1 Aug. 1783.

[5] Captain John Archdeacon (see below).

[6] Captain John Archdeacon, Cadet in 1768, made Capt. 4 Jan. 1781, 1st Bengal Sepoys, was killed at Seringapatam 6 Feb. 1792 (Hodson, *List of Officers*, i. 46; Dodwell and Miles,

and by the month of February next I hope to be able to send you a Bill for fifty pounds at Least.

The Allowances[7] I receive[8] now will enable me not only to remit this sum, but to make a like present to my Dear Mother every year while I remain out of the Company's provinces, or in the Field.

Nothing will ever afford me more pleasure than contributing everything in my power towards making you and my Dear Brothers and Sisters happy.

I am now studying the Persian language[9] and already have made some progress in it. Indeed I do not neglect a single opportunity to improve myself, nor would my Friends admit of it was I so inclined.

Pray give my love to Nancy and my old Nurse[10] and believe me to be Your affectionate Son,

Francis Coleridge

22–3). He acted like a 'second father' to Frank. *Post* No. 21, Capt. John Archdeacon to Ann Bowdon Coleridge, 12 Nov. 1784.

[7] 'allo' del.   [8] 'ha' del.

[9] On studying Persian, *Ante* No. 3, John Coleridge to William Coleridge, 29 Sept. 1774; *post* No. 22, John Coleridge to George Coleridge, 1 Dec. 1784; No. 24, John Coleridge to James Coleridge, 12 Aug. 1785.

[10] Molly Newbery. *Post* No. 26, Francis Coleridge to Anne Coleridge, 29 Oct. 1785.

Capt. John Archdeacon[1] to Ann Bowdon Coleridge

12 NOVEMBER 1784

Lucknow,[2] Nov. 12, 1784

Madam:

The interest I have in Mr Coleridge's[3] welfare, and in everything that concerns him induces me to take a liberty which I am persuaded cannot be disagreeable to a parent fond of a Son every way worthy of her tenderest affection.

Since Mr Coleridge's arrival in the Country he has been attached to the Corps I command, and for some time past has been immediately under my own particular charge. It is with pleasure I inform you, that his amiable Manners, and good Disposition has already, young as he is, preserved him the esteem of a respectable set of Gentlemen who have every inclination to push him forward in the World at a proper period.

I am a stranger to the contents of the accompanying Letter from my little pupil,[4] but I doubt not the goodness of his Heart is visible in it, tho' perhaps expressed in a stile which may require time and application to polish. Indeed my young Friend hinted to me how very agreeable it would be to him to make you a Remittance, and that he would communicate his desire of doing it as soon as possible. It shall be my care that this Intention be carried into execution, nor will he, I am persuaded, ever neglect a parent, whom Inclination and Duty, so early in life, leads him to assist.

I congratulate you, Madam, on having a dutiful and affectionate Son, who promises fair to be a credit to his Family, and a comfort to you when he returns to his native Climate.

I am Madam, Your very obedient, humble servant,

J Archdeacon

[1] *Ante* No. 20, Francis Coleridge to Ann Bowdon Coleridge, 10 Nov. 1784, n. 6.
[2] The same place from which Frank wrote to his mother two days previously (No. 20).
[3] Frank's.
[4] Almost certainly No. 20, dated two days before. Frank was 14.

John Coleridge to George Coleridge

1 DECEMBER 1784

Barrampore,[1] near Calcutta, Dec. 1, 1784

My dear George,

I have received your kind letters of the 20th of March and the 1st of April, and the perusal of them gave me more pleasure and happiness than I can find words to express. I thank my God for granting such health and spirits to our dear Mother, may she long continue to possess both, so that her latter days may be a scene of tranquility and happiness. From your pleasing account of the Family I think with a little exertion on all sides we may do very well. My little hero Frank is at present a great distance from me, but his situation is an excellent one, for he is under the command of a very particular intimate and friend of mine[2] and in the receipt of considerable pay and allowances which will in all likelyhood enable him by this time next year to render a considerable assistance to the Family, indeed I believe the youngster is considerably above the World already, that is I mean for a lad of his years and standing. He is at present studying the Persian with the greatest attention,[3] and let me assure you, my friend, that he promises as fair for being a good Soldier and a sensible man as any boy I ever saw in my life. I have enclosed Nancy's and James' letters to him but[4] have not as yet received an answer from him.

I have since I wrote home last been rather unfortunate. A friend of mine was in distress for Cash to clear himself of a disgraceful business he had got into at Surat, he applied to me for assistance, and I granted him the needfull.[5] About 4 months after this affair happened he was taken Ill from the severity of a long March, and died, he left me his sole Executor with an idea thus that I might repay myself from the sale of his effects, however there has been a Bond debt presented

---

[1] Berhampore, 100 miles north of Calcutta.

[2] Capt. John Archdeacon.

[3] *Ante* No. 20, Francis Coleridge to Ann Bowdon Coleridge, 10 Nov. 1784, n. 9.

[4] 'An'? del.

[5] The 'needfull' is probably the full amount of debt, but could refer to interest only. Details of this affair are unknown, but John gave money freely, including the large sum of £1000 to James, and also 900 rupees (about £80) to one 'Mrs Lewis' (Nos. 31, 40) shortly before he died, his estate insolvent.

against the Estate that will I am very apprehensive sweep away every farthing of the amount of the Estate. This, George, is an unlucky hit, however don't say anything of it to the old Lady[6] as it might make her uneasy. I shall, please God, be able to bring up the Leeway in a very few months, the only point that makes me anxious is that 'tis a doubt whither I shall be able to make the remittance that I intended, but rest assured I shall strain every nerve to keep matters in the proper road.

I mett a Mr Dawes[7] the other day who speaks in the highest terms of you. He has, poor fellow, lost a Worthy Brother, if you know his friends you had better inform them of the Accident. As this letter goes by the first ship of the season, I shall not tire you with a long epistle, as so many other opportunities will offer during the season for writing you.

Make my duty to my Mother and my love to my Brothers, Uncles, Aunts etc., and further tell my lovely amiable Nancy that I will answer her letters by the next ship; the sweet creature; I don't know, George how it is but that innocent girl takes up more of my thoughts than you can conceive.

Accept the love and friendship of your affectionate friend and Brother,

John Coleridge

[6] Their mother Ann, now 57.

[7] Possibly Robert Dawes (d. 1803), Capt. in 1778 and Major in 1784; but when John identifies 'Mr Dawes', presumably a civilian, this may be Henry Dawes, later Collector of Etawah, or Charles Dawes, later Magistrate of Midnapore (Hodson, *List of Officers*, ii. 28–9; *India Register*, i. 8–9), although these men did not begin their respective civil service careers in Bengal until 1801 and 1803. The brother who died is Thomas Dawes (1763–84), Cadet in 1781 and Lt. in 1782. He died at Rangpur on 24 Aug. 1784 (Dodwell and Miles, 80–1).

John Coleridge to Ann Bowdon Coleridge

12 AUGUST 1785

Address: To Mrs A Coleridge, Ottery S Mary.

Burrampore,[1] Bengall, Aug. 12, 1785

My dear Mother,

The enclosed letter[2] is for my worthy and affectionate Brother James by reading it you'll see how matters stand with me and the youngster[3] who is the very joy of my heart. The sooner you forward the letter to James the better, as his mind will not be perfectly easy 'till he receives it. To say anything in this would be repetition, so I have only to assure you my dear beloved Parent that 'tis my daily Prayer that you may be blessed with a long continuation of health and happiness and that I may one day have the pleasure of personally receiving your blessing.

Let me request you to give my respectful remembrance to all my Ottery friends and assure them that I retain the same affection and love for them that I ever did. If Nancy is present she'll smile I take it at a passage in James' letter.

Your affectionate and Dutifull son,

John Coleridge

[1] *Ante* No. 22, John Coleridge to George Coleridge, 1 Dec. 1784, n. 1.
[2] No. 24, John Coleridge to James Coleridge, 12 Aug. 1785, written the same day.
[3] Frank.

John Coleridge to James Coleridge

12 AUGUST 1785

Address: Capt. James Coleridge, the 6th Regt. Foot.

Burrampore Cantonments, Bengall, Aug. 12, 1785[1]

My dear James,

I have received yours of the 1st of Oct., 1784 from Dublin and the perusal of it gave me the highest satisfaction.[2] I thank you for the confidence you have put in me and depend upon it I will remitt you the needful by the very first opportunity that offers this season. Further I beg that you'll make my best thanks to the Gentlemen that may have stood your friends in this business and inform them that I should be happy in an opportunity of returning the obligation.

I should have sent you a very considerable sum a long time ago but was prevented by a Gentleman's death, in whose hands my little all was trusted and who upon inquiry has died Insolvent, so I lost every farthing I was worth, this was rather unlucky as we are circumstanced at present, but as the matter cannot be mended, I must endeavour to extricate myself without repining.[3] I have friends and very sincere ones, who are always ready to assist and support me, by this goodness and my own prudence I hope in 2 or 3 years to be capable of sending that assistance to my dear Mother and family that is incumbent upon every good man to do.

In remitting this £1000 I think I had better make the Bill payable to Mother, on her Order, in case you should be absent upon the arrival of the Bill in England you can mention what is to be done with the Cash on its being received. Francis writes me that he remitted £80 about six months ago, but you cannot as yet have received it, for the first Bill was lost in an accident happening to the Asburton Indiaman,[4] but he has no doubt taken care to send a Duplicate of the Bill by the

---

[1] '1784' del.

[2] All letters received by John and Frank in India have apparently been lost, though John's chest was sent home (*SDH* 44).

[3] *Ante* No. 22, John Coleridge to George Coleridge, 1 Dec. 1784. In nine months, John managed to accumulate £1000 to send to James, the amount stipulated by Capt. Biggs. This exceeded ten times Revd Coleridge's annual salary.

[4] A merchant vessel.

Packet that was despatched since. Frank is at present stationed at Cawnpore[5] about a 1000 miles distant from this place. He is under the Guardianship of my friend Capt. J Archdeacon,[6] a man of whose sense and virtue I have the highest opinion, indeed the youngster improves under him amazingly, and is beloved and esteemed by every person that knows him. He studys the Persian, and has made some proficiency in it, for in his last Letter he says that I shall never want a Persian interpreter when he has the pleasure of being with me again, so I think, James, the Boy promises fair for being a Shining Character.

What you mention concerning Luke must be seriously thought of,[7] I cannot at present render him the necessary assistance, but the moment it is in my power he shall hear from me. I don't like the conduct of Mr Buller,[8] his excusing himself by accusing his memory of a treachery for a breach of his Promise is all a Joke, good men never promise but to perform and virtue seldom or ever permitts the memory to fail. Your description of my dearest Sister,[9] made my Heart palpitate with joy and affection, may virtue and dignity be her Motto and strict honour the guardian of it is my prayer. If ever the Blind Goddess[10] should shower down her favours on me I will endeavour to put that dear helpless Girl in a Line that her virtue intended her to shine in. I received a tender affectionate Letter from her which I have not as yet mustered up resolution enough to answer, but I will do it by the next Ship. I received Letters from Ned, George, and Luke which were answered, but the letters were all lost I have been informed since, so I beg you'll inform them that I'm faultless. Do you know, James, that Nancy has got a kind of lover in this part of the world. My friend Capt: Meredith[11] is a little touched from the description you

[5] *Ante* No. 19, Francis Coleridge to Anne Coleridge, 25 Oct. 1784, n. 2.

[6] *Ante* No. 20, Francis Coleridge to Ann Bowdon Coleridge, 10 Nov. 1784, in which Frank also mentions studying Persian.

[7] Probably Luke's entering medical training about a year earlier, and the expenses associated with it.

[8] Sir Francis Buller (1746–1800), third son of James and a highly esteemed judge, had been a boarder at the King's School under Revd John Coleridge and had lived in the Coleridge home (*DNB*). He obtained from John Way the nomination for STC to enter Christ's Hospital in 1782 (Chambers, 3, 6–7). The conduct and promise alluded to by John are unidentified. Buller later made the infamous remark that a man might beat his wife provided the stick be no thicker than his thumb (*LAO* 166).

[9] Anne (Nancy), who was working at a milliner's in Exeter.

[10] Dike in Greek legend but generally represented by the Roman deity Astraea, goddess of justice, blindfolded and holding a twin-pan scale.

[11] John Meredith (d. 1786), Cadet in 1769, made Capt. 7 Jan. 1781, and in charge of 1st Bengal Regt. in 1782 (Hodson, *List of Officers*, ii. 282; Dodwell and Miles, 174–5, which

have given of her. We have lived as Brothers together for many years, and I may say few Brothers have a more mutual affection for each other. I have been thinking for these some days of getting Sam a couple of years hence sent out to me as a Cadet at the India House.[12] Let me know your sentiments upon this scheme in your next. If you should by accident ever meet a Colonel Bailie[13] or a Major James Dickson[14] of this service, make yourself known to them, they are very particular friends of mine. Well, James, I will now bid you farewell for a month, when you shall hear from me again. God bless and protect you.

Your affectionate friend and Brother,

John Coleridge

does not record the death). His death was a blow to John (*post* No. 35, Francis Coleridge to Anne Coleridge, 1 Nov. 1788).

[12] John had earlier thought that General Goddard would provide for STC. His present scheme was not the only nor the least of family efforts to enter STC into the military (*post* No. 28, George Coleridge to Ann Bowdon Coleridge, bef. 11 May 1786).

[13] William Bailie, made Lt. Col. in E. India Co. Army in 1775. He died in captivity at Seringapatam in 1792.

[14] James Dickson (1744–1829), Cadet in 1768, Capt. in 1778, and Major in 1784 (Hodson, *List of Officers*, ii. 61).

John Coleridge to *Anne Coleridge*

2 OCTOBER 1785

Address: To Miss A Coleridge at Ottery S Mary, near
Exeter, Devon

Burrampore,[1] Oct. 2, 1785

My dearest Sister,

I had the great pleasure of receiving three days ago your tender and affectionate letter of July 1784 and since the Period I may safely say that I have perused it 20 times, the delicate and soft sentiments that shine through the whole of it, added to the justness of your Ideas upon your present situation[2] has given me a perfect knowledge of the virtuous mind of the writer. Yes, my much beloved Nancy, your letter has convinced me that you are everything I could wish. I do not flatter you when I inform you that you have not only made me happy but that I pride myself in being possessed of a Sister that bears so beautifull a mind. You call me in your letter your brother unknown and justly so, but in future I must request you'll when you write me conceive you are personally acquainted with me, equally as much so as with James or any other of my good Brothers, that have the happiness of seeing and conversing with you. When I was about to leave Europe you was an infant, and many is the time, my Nancy, I have had you in my arms and gazed at you with pleasure and affection, tho' at that period people in general thought I was an obstinate hard-hearted boy that had neither feeling nor affection, but I think I may modestly say they judged without their Host.

I have now one fault to find with you, which is, that you rated every trifling natural act of mine in too high and particular a manner. I have not as yet done anything like what my friends have a right to expect from me, but by the blessing of God if my unfortunate <   >[3] do not always pursue me, I will fulfill their warmest wishes. My late misfortune has thrown me back a little in the world, but my Rank and prospects are such, that I expect to be enabled by this time next year

---

[1] *Ante* No. 22, John Coleridge to George Coleridge, 1 Dec. 1784.
[2] She was living and working in Exeter, apparently as a milliner's shop assistant.
[3] *SDH* 41 prints 'Fates'.

to render my dear beloved Parent and the rest of the Family that yearly assistance I intended. What at present troubles me is whither I shall be able to make up this Season the remittance for James for since I wrote him I have met with a disappointment, although no loss in the money way. However I shall exert my best endeavours and if I should in some degree prove unsuccessful, I hope his generous friends will rest contented till next Season.

I have sent Frank his letters, which will no doubt make him happy. His conduct is so highly praiseworthy that he is an honour to his Family, indeed he is beloved and honoured by every person that knows him. I shall have the pleasure of seeing him in about two months, and a joyful meeting it will be; poor little fellow, I have been absent from him now near 14 months; his Corps is coming down to Calcutta, which I am in some degree happy at, altho' it will be a loss to him as to Cash, but he will have an opportunity of seeing a great deal of the first Company in India, which will polish him and give him a proper confidence, without which nothing is to be got or had in these degenerate days.

O, I had like to have forgot to thank you for your kind and much valued present, it now adorns my bosom, and it frequently, very frequently reminds me of the much beloved person, who was the owner of it.[4]

If you should at any time by accident see my old Nurse,[5] you must say everything for me to her that you conceive will please her. If it ever shall be my fortune to visit my native land,[6] I will, after having received the blessing and embraces of my much honoured Parent, go and visit her be she where she will, for I am under very great obligations to her. O my dear Girl, you can have no conception of that woman's kindness and attention to me. I have known her when some trifling accident has happened to me show all the tenderness and feeling of a Parent and when I have been about to leave her to return to my Parents I have observed the large tear run down her aged Face and her countenance too well expressed the pain which she felt at parting with me. O Butterfly! Butterfly![7] how many were the happy

----

[4] This may refer to 'Nancy's Picture in miniature', requested by John two years earlier (*ante* No. 13, John Coleridge to James Coleridge, 1 Aug. 1783).

[5] Molly Newbery, now in her late forties.

[6] The word 'native' would resonate in STC's 'Dear native Brook!' to open 'Sonnet to the River Otter' and, recalling the trip to London after his father's death, in 'torn / By early sorrow from my native seat' in his farewell sonnet to Christ's Hospital.

[7] *SDH* 43 prints 'Butterley', which is clearly correct.

innocent hours I past there; if you should ever have occasion to pass near the place, visit it for my sake, and if an old large Ash Tree still stands at the bottom of the Green,[8] station yourself under it, and just reflect that you are standing on the spot where I some 20 years ago used to exert all my endeavours to rise the first in the Athletic exercises, while the good old woman used to stand and shudder for every single bruise I might receive, and tenderly chide me when I got home for contending with lads above my age and size. I don't know, Sister, whither this subject yeilds[9] you any entertainment, but the reflections I have[10] on[11] it frequently gives me the most pleasing sensations.

I must now think of concluding for were I to go on writing or rather conversing with you I should fill more paper than the Post would choose to carry, so make my most dutifull love to my dear Mother, and tell her that the news of her being in health and spirits gives joy and pleasure to my heart, and for a continuation of which she has my daily prayers. I shall write Luke by the next Ship, this letter goes in the Governor's Packet, no small favour I assure you, and it was by mere accident I heard of the opportunity. Make my love to my Brothers, for God knows I love and esteem them. Well I must now relieve you from reading this scrawl which I have been forced [to] run[12] through in a hurry.

I have only one thing more to add, which is that I pray that the great protector of Innocence and Virtue will defend and guard you in every situation in life, and I am my much beloved Nancy, your affectionate Brother and friend,

John Coleridge

[8] 'The old ash-tree at Butterleigh is gone, the green is now the school-yard' (*SDH* 44).
[9] For 'yields'.   [10] 'frequently' del.   [11] 'of it' del.
[12] The transcript reads 'forced run'.

No. 26

Francis Coleridge to *Anne Coleridge*

29 OCTOBER 1785

Dinapore,[1] Oct. 29, 1785

My dear Nancy,

It is impossible to express what an addition your letter was to the pleasures of Christmas day, for it happened to arrive on the very day that we were celebrating the Nativity of our Blessed Saviour.

Give me leave, my dear Sister, to apologise to you for not mentioning in my last letter those virtuous Benefactors of our Family[2] whose generous hands have made the load of misery sit easy on us and our dear and only Parent. Do, Nancy, do, my dear girl tell Mrs Hart's family how I love, how I respect them, and that my little heart is ready to burst in gratitude towards them. Give, Nancy, a kiss for my sake.

I hope my dear Mother still continues to enjoy a good state of health. It is my constant prayer to heaven that the remaining part of her life may glide away smoothly and happily, and that there may be no more scenes of distress and misery [to][3] rack the breast of he[4] to whom I owe my existence.

I have the pleasure of sending home by Captain Waugh[5] a friend of mine a Bill of one hundred pounds as a present to my dear Mother. He will forward it to you as soon as he arrives in England and you will send to our Mother. It is the saving out of my pay since my Brother and I have been ordered to Different Brigades, which has been about

[1] Dinajpur, in Bangladesh, north of Calcutta. The opening sentence suggests that the date may be a slip for 29 Dec.

[2] The Hart family of Exeter, visited by Revd John Coleridge the evening before he died. While working in Exeter Anne may have lived with them. Sara Hart married Luke Herman and in 1796 her sister Jane married George Coleridge; her first fiancé William Coleridge had died sixteen years earlier on the eve of their wedding day. The Hart family, vital to Anne and the Coleridge brothers, first provided the sister–sister to brother–brother pattern of relationships that came to dominate STC's life. *Post* No. 35, Francis Coleridge to Anne Coleridge, 1 Nov. 1788; No. 36, Francis Coleridge to Ann Bowdon Coleridge, 20 Sept. 1791. See Introd., pp. 6, 15.

[3] [B].   [4] for 'her'?

[5] George Waugh, Cadet in 1769 and Capt. on 16 Nov. 1780. He was finally struck off in 1793 after having returned to England (Dodwell and Miles, 266–7; *post* No. 30, George Waugh to Ann Bowdon Coleridge, 23 Aug. 1786).

these two years. Lately the Corps he was in relieved the Regt to which I belong. We had a meeting, I do not exaggerate, Nancy, when I tell you it was as tender and affectionate as when we first met at Bombay; when we parted tears flow'd on both sides, but we were Soldiers, and as a Soldier I was forced to leave him and march with my Regt; he is in fine health, though the situation of affairs at home has made him rather melancholy.

And now for my good, my dear and faithful Molly[6] (What—before Brothers and Sisters for shame Frank, I think I hear you say: yes, Nancy for I am sorry to say I lay under more obligations to that good woman than I do to all the Brothers and Sisters I have got except my Secundum Pater John). Assure her of my unalterable affection and love towards her, that she is still as dear to me as ever, and that I shall ever recollect her goodness to me when I was at home, for who else would ever wipe the tear off little Frank's cheek, and comfort him in any little distress or sickness; poor as she was she never refused me any little money that I might have wanted. No, her generous soul gave even before I asked. Desire my mother to give her five Guineas out of the Hundred pounds I have sent, that is, if she can conveniently spare them, for when Poor Molly has had but a penny in the world she would divide it with me, and doth not Gratitude demand something in return, certainly, little as it is. When she knows it comes from me she will think it thousands and when the Recording Angel gives in a list of my crimes, I hope my Ingratitude will never be numbered amongst them, for I hold that of all Crimes in the utmost detestation and abhorrence, and the man that can be guilty of Ingratitude let him die the death of a Dog, and even that in my opinion is too good for him.

Remember me to Maria,[7] I ought to say something more, but as I have not room I hope she will excuse me. Remember me to all my Brothers, Sisters, Uncles, Aunts, Cousins and Friends, and now give me leave to conclude with Being, My Dear Nancy, Your affectionate and Handsome Brother,

Francis Coleridge

Do you know I'm grown very handsome, tell Maria so.

[6] Molly Newbery.
[7] Maria Northcote (*ante* No. 19, Francis Coleridge to Anne Coleridge, 25 Oct. 1784).

Francis Coleridge to Ann Bowdon Coleridge

27 JANUARY 1786

Address: To Mrs Coleridge, Ottery S Mary, Devon; Recommended to the care of Messr Wm Paxton and Co.[1]

Patna,[2] Jan. 27, 1786

My dear Mother,

Inclosed I have the pleasure of sending you an order for one hundred pounds. Happy should I have been if I could make it two, but my situation is now altered, being ordered into the Company's provinces, where I only receive about one third of my former allowances. However my Brother is gone up into the Country where his income will be considerably increased.

Believe me to be, my Dear[3] Mother, your very Affectionate and Dutifull son,

Francis Coleridge

I will write to you very fully shortly nor must you consider this letter in any other light than as one upon Business. My endeavours shall be exerted My dear Mother to send you more of the same nature when in my power.

[1] 'Paxton and Elder, Wine Merchants, York Bldg, Buckingham St., Strand' (*Baldwin's New and Complete Guide to All Concerned with Trade . . . London* (1770), 155). *Post* No. 29, Wm Paxton and Co. to Ann Bowdon Coleridge, 9 Aug. 1786.
[2] In Bihar, about 100 miles south of Nepal.   [3] 'de' del.

George Coleridge to Ann Bowdon Coleridge

BEFORE 11 MAY 1786

[Before May 11, 1786][1]

Dearest Mother,

I received your letter and Mr Smerdon's.[2] Inclosed you will find the Certificate, which I would have you get filled up as soon as possible. My Uncle got it for you. I think you had better send it inclosed in a Frank to the Doctor, who being immediately on the spot may get an earlier Payment. He[3] is very well recovered, if Inattention to himself does not again throw him back. We should come down about the 21st of May, but what is the use? Here he can spend his Time with great advantage, and little Expence. His Aunt[4] has not received her money yet. I suppose he owes her about ten Pounds. I must endeavour to manage it somehow or other. However that cannot be till I return from the Country again. His Hair Dresser, Launderers and some others must be paid. He is, I assure you, in great Repute, and is much noticed by the First Men in the Town in the Physical way. I thought I gave you lately a long account of Sam, the reason he could not get in to the List, and how unnecessary all our Applications on that head had been.[5] I saw him last week, he was very well and said he had written two or three Letters, and had expected some answer, but had received none.

If I visit Ottery this time, it will not be till the 11th of May, which will be on a Thursday. It is a Week later than I expected it. If anything alters my Intentions, I will give you Notice of it some time before. Should it be the Case, I hope I shall not forget the Tea Commissions ac.[6] I must beg that Nancy be there by the Time I come home.[7] I

---

[1] Pencil in another hand.

[2] Then Vicar of St Mary's Church. *Ante* No. 18, Luke Herman Coleridge to Ann Bowdon Coleridge, 18 Oct. 1784.

[3] Apparently Luke Herman, at London Hospital; possibly STC (Chambers, 13).

[4] Aunt Short, sister of Ann Coleridge and John Bowdon, the uncle mentioned in the third sentence.

[5] STC could not get into the List because he was not yet 16. *Ante* No. 5, Robert Hamilton to Revd John Coleridge, 20 Dec. 1775. The family had apparently made a number of attempts to enlist STC, then 13. See Introd., p. 13.

[6] for 'account'?   [7] Nancy had been working and living in Exeter.

propose taking a great deal of Trouble with her, as I probably at some Future Time shall bring down an accomplished Girl as her companion for a month. It is a young Lady of elegant Accomplishments and lovely Disposition that I am in Love with, but no very great Fortune. I suppose by your Account Mrs Collins is a greater Acquisition to Ottery than the Captain.[8] He will find it necessary shortly to act as you Ottery people do, which I think is in general very rational. I have not time to write you a longer Letter. My love to the Hodges,[9] Smerdons. Remember me to Wright and Wife, and Compliments to <   > if you please. I am sorry Patty Ripp is unwell.[10] Love to her.

Your very affectionate son,

G. Coleridge

Doctor is rather hurt to think you have forgot his Honor pledged that he did not carry on any correspondence with Maria[11] either directly or indirectly.

[8] Possibly the wife of Stephen Collins, S. Gloucestershire Reg. Foot (*Army List* (1786), 25), but he is listed as Lt. not Capt.

[9] STC knew the Hodges and mentions Mrs Hodge to his brother George on 13 Jan. 1793 (*CL* i. 47). The Smerdons are Vicar Fulwood Smerdon and his wife.

[10] 'uni' del. The Wrights and Patty Ripp are untraced.

[11] Maria Short, George's cousin. It might be considered a breach of etiquette for a bachelor to write to an unmarried young lady unless they were engaged. Two years later Maria Short marries 'a Mr Turner' (*post* No. 34, George Coleridge to Ann Bowdon Coleridge, 23 May 1788); or George's postscript may refer to financial arrangements.

No. 29

Wm Paxton and Co.[1] to *Ann Bowdon Coleridge*

9 AUGUST 1786

Address: Mrs Coleridge, Ottery S Mary, Devon

Buckingham Street, London, 9th August, 1786

Madam:

Inclosed we send you a Letter we received from our House at Calcutta, who desired us to assist you in negotiating the Bill inclosed for £100.[2] You'll please therefore return it to us with your name wrote on the back of it, and we shall send it to Wakefield for Acceptance. When we inform you of its being accepted and paid we shall either remit the money to you or desire you to draw on us for it.

We are, Madam, your most obedient servants,

Wm Paxton and Co.

[1] *Ante* No. 27, Francis Coleridge to Ann Bowdon Coleridge, 27 Jan. 1786, n. 1.
[2] The Bill sent by Francis on 27 Jan. 1786.

George Waugh to *Ann Bowdon Coleridge*

23 AUGUST 1786

Address: Mrs Coleridge, Ottery S Mary, Devonshire

Wakefield,[1] Aug. 23, 1786

Madam:

Inclosed you will receive an order on Raikes and Co[2] for One Hundred Pounds payable at ten days, which you will transmit for their acceptance and which sum you will please to receive when due. It is the amount of cash received from your son Francis Coleridge ere my departure from India and which he desired might be paid to you.[3] I left him a Bill for the amount on my Father payable at 90 days sight which, when you receive please to let me have it. Business I expect will draw me towards Ottery in a few weeks, when I propose myself the pleasure of seeing you, until which I wish you health and am your very obedient humble servant,

Geo: Waugh

N.B. My Father acquaints me that he has just received an address from your son Mr Geo: Coleridge respecting the Bill. You will please to make known to him (with my compliments) that I have settled the transaction with you and you will oblige me by acknowledging the receipt of the accompanying Bill. Geo: Waugh

[1] *Ante* No. 29, Wm Paxton and Co. to Ann Bowdon Coleridge, 9 Aug. 1786. Frank's Bill was sent to Wakefield for payment.

[2] William Raikes, a director on the Exchange, was earlier with Crown Co., Threadneedle St. (*Baldwin's Guide*, 161).

[3] *Ante* No. 26, Francis Coleridge to Anne Coleridge, 29 Oct. 1785, where Frank names Capt. (George) Waugh as the person to whom he gives the Bill.

No. 31

Mrs Lewis[1] to *Capt. John Archdeacon*

26 SEPTEMBER 1787

Tillicherry,[2] 26th Sept., 1787

Dear Captain Archdeacon:

Our friend Coleridge[3] came to this place on the 25th January last[4] in a very bad state of health.[5] It is with great concern I am to inform you that notwithstanding the best medical assistance in our power was afforded him, he was never able to leave it again except for a short trip down the Coast, but departed this life on the 7th of April[6] since when I have not had an opportunity of a direct conveyance to Calcutta, however one now offering I embrace it to send you your boy Jack, or, as he calls himself Senulla.[7] As I do not know who is administrator or executor to Coleridge I have taken the liberty of forwarding his chest containing all the effects he had here as per enclosed list, by this vessel, to your address, and shall be much obliged to you to inform his administrator or executor that I have about nine hundred rupees which I borrowed of Coleridge about a month before his death now in my hands,[8] which I am ready to pay whomsoever he or they shall appoint to receive it. Senulla has behaved exceeding well ever since Coleridge died.

I am, with great truth, dear Archdeacon, yours very sincerely,

[no signature]

[1] Mrs Lewis, untraced. *Post* No. 40, Charles Close to F. G. Coleridge, 26 Jan. 1836.
[2] 'Bengal' del. Tillicherry is in Kerala, north of Calicut (Kozhikode).
[3] John Coleridge.
[4] Because of confusion over the date of John's death, this should be noted as 25 Jan. 1787.
[5] He may have had malaria.
[6] On the date of John's death, see below, p. 94.
[7] Senulla: 'army chief'.
[8] On John's estate and administrator, see below, p. 94.

Captain S. Earle[1] to Ann Bowdon Coleridge

15 APRIL 1788

Address: Mrs Coleridge, St Mary Ottery

Stokeley, April 15, 1788

Madam:

I have lately received a Letter from the East Indies, dated in August last from a very particular friend of mine (Capt Archdeacon) who begs me to make application to you to inquire if you received £100 which your Son Frank remitted to you (a Bill on Mr Waugh at 3 months sight) requesting me if the Cash has not been paid to write Mr Waugh on the subject which I will most readily do. I make no doubt but the Money will be immediately paid.[2]

Capt: Archdeacon gave me the melancholy intelligence of the Death of your eldest Son. He died in April last at Tillicherry,[3] I doubt not but your Son Frank has made you acquaint[ed] with it ere this. He (Frank) has lived with Capt: Archdeacon for several years who is as careful of Him, as if He were a Child of His own. He is a very worthy young Man and esteemed by every person who has the pleasure of His acquaintance, you would not know Him. He is so much grown. I saw Him on His first arrival in India and two years ago when I last saw Him, He was quite a Man. He is still an Ensign, but if, please God, he lives I have no doubt but that He will do very well.[4] He is a very different turn of mind from Jack. He, poor lad, was too generous ever to save anything for Himself, but if I mistake not Frank will always live and act like a Gentleman, without being too extravagant.[5] I was well acquainted with them both. Frank was at Barrampore about 100 miles above Calcutta last April in very good health.

---

[1] Capt. Solomon Earle attained that rank on 21 Aug. 1779, and was struck off in 1793 (Dodwell and Miles, 94–5).

[2] The Bill mentioned in earlier correspondence (Nos. 26, 27, 29, 30).

[3] This helps confirm the date of John's death as April 1787 (see below, p. 94).

[4] Frank was promoted to Lt. on 5 June 1790.

[5] John loaned money to others in India. *Ante* No. 22, John Coleridge to George Coleridge, 1 Dec. 1784; No. 31, Mrs. Lewis to Capt. Archdeacon, 26 Sept. 1787. He also freely sent James the large sum for his captaincy.

I am, Madam, your most obedient Humble Servant,

S Earle

My direction is as follows
Capt. S. Earle, Stokeley
near Dartmouth

George Coleridge to Ann Bowdon Coleridge

26 APRIL 1788

Hackney, April 26, 1788

My dearest Mother,

If there be any Comfort which can be afforded you besides Heaven, and a clear conscience on this melancholy event it is that you have a Son now addressing you—who Feels more for your Distress than his own, who will feel himself doubly bound to fill up that Tenderness and filial Affection which you have lost in a Son[1] who was great and *good*. Think that each one of your children will make you, if possible a Gainer by your Loss. Believe me, my dear Mother, I felt a very sensible Relief, as soon as I had perused the melancholy circumstance, that it was not *you*. For I had almost anticipated it at the opening of my dear James' Letter, whose Tenderness to you as well as that of all of us will be ever near you, whenever it is most wanted. Sorry am I that my Friends having interested themselves so much in my behalf should have rendered my stay in Town necessary; the Bishop indeed with great reluctance at last complied, and I must complete the Business if possible. My dear Ann[2] shall hear from me soon; she claims much of my Affection and Attention, and she shall not be disappointed. I beg you both to consider this common Lot of Humanity as Christians, to give to Sorrow that which Nature demands, and to permit the Arguments of Reason and Religion to have their full force. Those Arguments we are to seek for, and the God of all Comfort and Mercy will render them effectual, most probably with a Benediction, that such adversity only and such Resignation to it could have procured. I am inclined to think, my dear Mother, that you have those requisites about you which will make you reflect becomingly on the Event and from an Evil produce great good.[3]

---

[1] 'John Coleridge who died on the coast of Bombay in May 1786' [B]. Bernard Lord Coleridge was to revise the death date, below, p. 94. He takes this date from *post* No. 35, Francis Coleridge to Anne Coleridge, 1 Nov. 1788.

[2] Anne (Nancy), also mentioned in the postscript.

[3] The tenor of the letter and consolation suggests Ann Coleridge may have been aware that John's death was a suicide. *Post* No. 35, Francis Coleridge to Anne Coleridge, 1 Nov. 1788.

I suppose you have received the Paper I sent, and you see by it when it is to be paid.

In addition to the kind attention of Mrs Hodge[4] to you, I could wish Jenny Hart[5] to be with you a little. I wrote Mr Smerdon[6] lately and desired him to transfer a Bill of £2·5·6 which I had paid for him to you.

May God bless you with all Comfort, and under his Wing you cannot be unhappy; be assured of the sincere Affection and Duty of your Son,

G Coleridge

My kindest Love to Ann, and Mrs Hodge. James who will be with you shortly <   > will write me.

[4] Mrs Hodge, see *ante* No. 28, n. 9.
[5] George Coleridge and Jenny Hart married in 1796. In 1780 she had been engaged to William, who died on the eve of their wedding day.
[6] *Ante* No. 18, Luke Herman Coleridge to Ann Bowdon Coleridge, 18 Oct. 1784.

George Coleridge to *Ann Bowdon Coleridge*

23 MAY 1788

Mill Street, Hanover Square, May 23, 1788

My dear Mother,

I should not have neglected you thus long had I not been really and necessarily impeded, I have at last completed My Ordination Business, much to my Satisfaction and hope the Issue will be a real comfort to us all. The Day after my taking Orders I was taken a little oddly in my Head, but a good bleeding and an emetic by itself without anything to drink with it—I hope has carried it off again. Be assured I am very careful and attentive to myself, but none of you ever write me. Nancy should, and Mrs Hodge will, my direction is No. 7 Mill Street Hanover Square, Westminster, where I shall be about a week after your receiving this Letter, when I shall return to Hackney, with increas'd Business on my Hands. Pray let me have a Letter before I leave this place. Maria Short is married to a Mr Turner,[1] a Surveyor of good Business and Fortune; has settled £50 per ann: on her for Life. Your Brother is in a sad state.[2] Mrs Bishop says she shall never be happy without seeing you. Sam grows very tall, and I think handsome. He is a charming young man.[3]

I have inclosed the £10. I could wish to have added another to it. Were it in my Power, you know I would gladly do it, it *may* be however shortly. My Clerical Dress will cost me £9, besides taking Orders, Lodging and Living in Town, and many other little expenses unavoidable in my situation.

I beg I may hear soon how everything goes on. You know we are not born always to wear sorrow[4] on our Countenance: 'tis good that we *feel* sometimes, indeed it leaves us leisure to be good, and we are

---

[1] George's cousin married presumably A. R. Turner, 'estate surveyor' from Kent, the only Turner in the profession in or near London at this time (Peter Eden (ed.), *Dictionary of Land Surveyors . . . 1550–1850* (Folkestone: Dawson, 1975–6), 254).

[2] John Bowdon. *Ante* No. 10, William Coleridge to Ann Bowdon Coleridge, 31 July 1780. George may refer to ill-health or to John Bowdon's penchant for drink.

[3] STC, aged 15, was that year made a Grecian at Christ's Hospital. 'On the whole Coleridge may have been happier during the last years of his school life than at any other period, except possibly a brief one at Stowey' (Chambers, 13).

[4] 'su' del.

taught moreover to set our Affections[5] on things above: to be too much distress'd at any thing that may happen here below is unworthy a Xian.

Love to Nancy and Mrs Hodge. Believe me your very dutifully and affectionate,

G. Coleridge

[5] 'G' del.

Francis Coleridge to Anne Coleridge

1 NOVEMBER 1788

Camp at Burawgaun,[1] Nov. 1, 1788

[No salutation]

Perhaps long before my dear Sister receives this its office will have been performed or many melancholy Epistles[2] must have miscarried. When I received your very affectionate letter dated Feb: 1788 I was distressed beyond measure at finding it once more necessary to write[3] on a subject in itself how ungrateful to a Brother, in its consequences how afflicting to a Parent, and Sister and thro' every link of our Family Chain. My Nancy, my amiable and all affectionate Sister, if you are in presence of my Mother, retire before you turn to the Page. And now know, if unknown before, that you have but one Brother in India and that in May 1786[4] on the coast of Bombay, the dearest friend of my Nancy terminated his life, and rejoined his more than Brother Capt: Meredith[5] to part no more. After whose death he daily declined, and was advised by the Faculty to try the Sea air, the result—but I can say no more. If my Nancy has already felt it [it] would be unnecessary, if not 'twould be cruel. And permit me, my dear and only Sister to drop a subject so affecting for me to meditate on and too interesting[6] for your Happiness to peruse.

I still continue with my second father Captain Archdeacon who has been presented by Lord Cornwallis[7] with the command of a Sepoy or

---

[1] The locale is untraced. It may be a mistransliteration for Burdwan, 55 miles north-west of Calcutta.

[2] These letters, presumably written by Frank, have not survived and may not have reached England.

[3] Since Nancy had not known of John's death in Feb. 1788, but George wrote to their mother of it on 26 Apr. (No. 33), news of it must have reached the family during the intervening time.

[4] Frank may state the incorrect date, which was in all probability Apr. 1787 (see below n. 5; p. 94).

[5] *Ante* No. 24, John Coleridge to James Coleridge, 12 Aug. 1785. Capt. Meredith died in 1786. It is conceivable that John did die in May 1786, for 'he daily declined' after Capt. Meredith died. But since the date of Meredith's death cannot be pinpointed, other evidence strongly indicates Apr. 1787 for John's death.

[6] 'interesting': almost certainly for 'distressing'.

[7] Charles, 1st Marquess (1738–1805), associated earlier with the American War of Independence, in which he had reluctantly accepted command, was appointed Governor General of India (1786) and Commander in Chief in Bengal.

Native Batallion now on an independent Command in the interiour parts of India; by his interest I have been appointed to his Batallion and thro' his assistance and Patronage enjoy every happiness this amenity can give. But what can the Son of such a Parent, what can the Brother of such a Sister enjoy, when the eve of the first is darkened by distress and the meridian of the last clouded by misfortune.

My Brothers, have I then no Brothers? imagination dwells on their once loved features, some have escaped, others have faded, but their forms still exist in my heart and their memory with unabated love still give delight to my Soul. That they are greatly altered in appearances I can judge from myself, and am certain I could appear without any danger of being recognised before every one of my Family. Don't too hastily dissent or deny the possibility of such an occurrence for reasons, and them glaring ones that I may one of these days bring in support of my supposition.

You mention a letter from Miss Maria Northcott[8] but I have never received any. Present her with the grateful Thanks of the poor exile. Inform Miss <   > how very sensible I am of her kind attention and how very Proud she made me by the few lines her goodness obliged me with.

Assure the amiable and generous Hart family of my most fervent gratitude, nor do I despair of one day seeing them Personally, that out of my own house the world contains none I love so well. I dreamt some time ago of having married,[9] Nancy, and as you know marriages are made in heaven, and dreams are said to descend from above, we are certainly intended for each other, and I have only to find out some of the treasures of Hindostan to enable me to return home and throw myself at her feet. Pray inform me what reception seriously, Nancy, you think I should meet with.

Desire my dear little Sam (a propos of little I am exactly five feet 11 inches and a half measured yesterday) to write me, and if his Pride enquires why, I don't think proper to commence a correspondence. Say a great deal in my favour about Duty, business, climate, situation, etc.[10]

    [8] Maria Northcote. *Ante* No. 14, Francis Coleridge to Ann Bowdon Coleridge, 1 Aug. 1783.
    [9] To Maria Northcote, his childhood sweetheart.
    [10] The tone of this paragraph catches both the attempted closeness and competition of Frank and STC. It is not known if STC wrote to Frank at this time (it would have been 1789 if he received the request) but he certainly did so in 1792, probably after having read what would be Frank's last letter home (No. 36), one literally 'prophesying war'. STC's

Great was the satisfaction I received from your account of my dear Luke, may he prosper as he deserves.

The goodness and Virtues of my affectionate and dear George's heart with the fine sense and abilities of his head[11] make me drop a tear on reflecting how contracted his sphere is for exerting them.

Were my dear Edward to guard his memory from treachery nor while every one of the family experiences his natural tenderness let an absent Brother sink to oblivion.

Inform my ever honoured Brother James that I still consider that moment the happiest of my life that will present me with the opportunity of draping my sword to him. And to my Mother, my all affectionate, and all tender Parent, tell her I am as I was and ever have been and ever shall be, gratefull, affectionate and Dutifull.

Direct to me as follows. Ensg. Francis Coleridge, c/o Capt: John Archdeacon, Bengal Infantry, India. And now my dear Sister the last not least in love, let me implore the favour and blessings of God on you, may he protect you from all harm and make you as Happy as the most affectionate Brother could wish.

As you did not mention my Molly,[12] I shall be silent, not indifferent.

Your ever affectionate Brother,

Francis Coleridge

Our Batallion marches from Burawgaun higher into the Country the 15th of February next.

only known letter to Frank thus reached India months after Frank's death (*CL* i. 41; *HBK* 28–30; Introd., pp. 11–12).

[11] The combination of 'heart' and 'head' became a favourite tag for STC (e.g. *BL* i. 152).

[12] Molly Newbery, mentioned in Frank's earlier letters, esp. *ante* No. 26, to Anne Coleridge, 29 Oct. 1785.

RECORDS OF JOHN COLERIDGE

After publication of *The Story of a Devonshire House* in 1905, Bernard Lord Coleridge made enquiries about John and Francis Coleridge to Sir Arthur Godley, Permanent Under-Secretary of State for India. About John he then wrote (MS 47556 fo. 31^b):

> Since writing my 'Story of a Devonshire
> House' I have received the following
> information in regard to John Coleridge from
> Sir Arthur Godley,[1] Permanent Under-Secretary
> of State for India.
>   John Coleridge
>   Dodwell and Miles[2] give dates[:]
>   Cadet 1770
>   Captain 28th Feb: 1781
>   Died Dec: 1787 at Tillicherry.
>   No cadet papers to give parentage.
>   No record of marriage or burial.
>   Administration to estate granted to June 1788, Alex: Colvin,[3]
>   agent for James
>   Dickson,[4] a bond creditor.
>   Estate insolvent Rs. 2094 being paid in part payment of bond.
> Coleridge

Note To shew how difficult it is to arrive at accuracy in dates, the death of John Coleridge is ascribed to three different dates on authority[:]

(1) In a letter from Mrs Lewis to Capt: Archdeacon [No. 31] dated from Tillicherry Sept 26, 1787, endorsed in letter No. 38 [No. 40] she speaks of John Coleridge having died on *April 7, 1787*

(2) In Letter No. 16 [No. 38] dated Nov: 1, 1788 Francis Coleridge gives the date as *May 1786*

(3) The records of the India Office give the date as *Dec: 1787*
I should prefer *April 7, 1787*.[5]

---

[1] Sir John Arthur Godley, Oxford BA, 1871, Barrister at Law, Lincoln's Inn, 1876, and appointed Permanent Under-Secretary of State for India in 1883 (Foster, *Alumni*, i. 533).

[2] Dodwell and Miles: see List of Short Titles.

[3] Alexander Colvin, 'merchant and agent, firm of Colvin and Co., Bengal' (*India Register*, 18).

[4] *Ante* No. 24, John Coleridge to James Coleridge, 12 Aug. 1785.

[5] The weight of evidence supports this preference. According to Frank (No. 35), John 'terminated his life' and the tone of the letters surrounding his death suggests suicide. He was insolvent, had recently lost his 'more than Brother' Capt. Meredith, was in ill health, and sending him to the coast to recover probably heightened his sense of isolation. He had been separated from Frank.

No. 36

Francis Coleridge to Ann Bowdon Coleridge

20 SEPTEMBER 1791

Lord Campden,[1] Sept. 20, 1791

My ever honoured, ever beloved Parent,

Your letter has woke me amidst[2] the Din of arms to all the softer feelings of Nature. My Mamma think not because you have not heard of me, that you have not been daily, nay hourly in my Mind. I call my Creator to witness I love you with such affection that does not despair of Equality with my Happier Brothers, but I cannot like them tell you so every month nor always every year. For these three years past I have been stationed nigh 1400 miles from Calcutta. And tho' promoted[3] and ordered the European Batallion at Bockampore, His Lordship[4] in Council ordered me to succeed to the first Vacancy in the Native Batallion up the Country. He is since summons me with twelve other Officers and 800 Sepoys to attend the Grand Army previous to his laying siege to Seringapatam, the Capital of the Mysore Tyrant.[5] Proud of such an honourable distinction I join him with ardour, and if Fortune Crowns my Wishes will scatter the Pearls of the Sultan at the feet of my Mamma. Mr Tomkins[6] lingers on board for any letter for we are falling into the Main Ocean from the Ganges. I can detain him no longer and must be concise. My health has never known disease. My character has never known a stain. My friends I have never lost. Enemies I have never made and happy I have ever been, except when, Mamma, you call me across the Ocean. God bless you, best of Parents, tell your Children that their absent Brother is what he ought to be, or if he has one fault it is that of being too Partial to the banks of the Ganges. Molly I kiss you! would you know your favourite Boy again; live and you shall see him. My Nancy would my tears relieve

---

[1] Presumably a camp named for Sir Charles, 1st Earl of Camden (1713–94), made Lord High Chancellor in 1766.

[2] 'ad' del. [3] Frank had been made Lt. on 5 June 1790.

[4] Lord Cornwallis. *Ante* No. 35, Francis Coleridge to Anne Coleridge, 1 Nov. 1788.

[5] Tipoo Sahib (1753–99), son of Hyder Ali, the most formidable opponent the British had encountered. He succeeded his father in 1782. Cornwallis battled twice at Seringapatam (Srirangapatnam), seat of the sultans of Mysore (now in S. Mysore State), in 1792 and 1799. After the second battle in Mar. 1799 Tipoo Sahib was compelled to cede half his dominions.

[6] Possibly Lt. Christopher Tomkins (*Commissioned Sea Officers*, iii. 921); 'Mr' was commonly used for officers, though in other instances Frank employs rank.

you,[7] I would forget the Soldier and be more than Brother. Amiable Sister, never, never can I forget you.

I have not time to pour out my Heart. I am writing amongst hundreds of Soldiers. But the Hart Family thro' every member divides my Soul. Mamma receive my Dutifull my eternal affection. On my knees I call for your blessing on Your ever Duteous Child,

Frans Coleridge

I write again from Madras.[8]

[7] Nancy was buried on 12 Mar. 1791 (*PR* ii. 1068*b*); here Frank seems aware only of her long, difficult consumptive illness. He may have received news of her death prior to his own suicide, three to four months after this letter.

[8] No later letter is known.

RECORDS OF FRANCIS
S. COLERIDGE

As a result of his enquiries (above, p. 94), Bernard Lord Coleridge
included this in the transcription (MS 47556 fo. 45):

> Since writing my 'Story of a Devonshire
> House' I have received the following
> information in regard to Francis Syndercombe
> Coleridge from Sir Arthur Godley Permanent
> Under-Secretary of State for India[:]
> > Francis Coleridge.
> > > Cadet 1782.
> > > Lieutenant 5th June 1790.
> > > Died 21 Jan: 1792 in the Carnatic.[1]
> > > No cadet papers, or record of marriage or burial.
> > > 20 Oct 1792. Administration (with paper writing annexed)
> > > > granted to Henry Trail.[2]
> > > Estate all paid away.

'Endebted to my God for my Life, for everything else to [(1)] Capt: Archdeacon,
I resign to him who made me the existence he bestowed, and every earthly
possession besides (except my Gold Ring) I leave to the kind Father of my
youth. My Gold Ring [(2)] Lt. Conway will favor my memory by accepting.
Campbell[3] will not smile over my grave, and Captain A[4] may say of those who
loved me another is departed. Dec 19. Sewanndroog.[5] [1791][6]
sp.[7] Francis Coleridge'

(1) Capt: John Archdeacon killed at Seringapatam 6th Feb.: 1792.
(2) Probably Capt: E. S. Conway killed at Benares. 10th Jan.: 1799.

---

[1] European name for the region including Mysore, SE. India between the eastern Ghats
and coast, now Karnataka.

[2] Untraced.

[3] Capt. John Campbell, who held that rank from 22 Aug. 1779, resigned 24 Dec. 1791,
five days after this note; less likely is Capt. John Campbell, made Capt. Mar. 1781 and later
untraced (Dodwell and Miles, 56–7).

[4] Captain Archdeacon.

[5] Now Siwan, between the Gandak and Ghazhara, north-west of Patna, and about 100
miles south of Nepal.

[6] 1791 is the date on the copy sent by India House (MS 47556 fo. 34).

[7] sp.: *sine prole*: without issue. This 'paper writing', the last known thing written by Frank,
seems both a will and a suicide note. Reports of his death vary; they concur that he shot
himself. STC believed he was delirious from working on the siege at Seringapatam and was
carelessly left alone by his attendant (Introd., p. 12). STC noted that his mother kept in her
possession a gold watch presented to Frank by Lord Cornwallis for bravery at the siege.
Bernard Lord Coleridge in *SDH* reports that it was said Frank, wounded at the siege, became
delirious and shot himself. The date and place of death in the India House records may be
in error; the date of John's death in the same records almost certainly is (see above, p. 94).

Charles Baring[1] to James Coleridge

6 APRIL 1794[2]

Exmouth, 6th April, 1794

Dear Sir:

In consequence of the Bill now depending in Parliament we have had several conversations about raising a Volunteer Company of One Hundred Men, and this morning I have taken the liberty of mentioning your name to Mr Eyre[3] as a very desirable person to command it. I don't know how it may suit your Engagements, but if the Thing be agreeable to yourself I would wish you to make immediate application to Mr Rolle[4] who has certainly the power of Nomination. You will be so good to say that *a friend* in Exmouth has Informed you such Company is about to be established. Should it not suit your other Engagements, I hope only that you will take my nomination for a mark of that sincere Esteem for your Character with which I have been Impressed and that you will believe me, Dear Sir, your obedient humble servant,

Charles Baring

Admrl Bowyer[5] with twelve sail of the Line gone from Torbay[6] this morning.

[1] Probably Charles (1742–1829), son of John Baring, an immigrant from Bremen who settled in Exeter in 1717 and became a prominent merchant and woollen manufacturer.

[2] One day later, 7 Apr., STC was given news of his release from the army, secured through George especially, but also James, whose star in the service was rising. This letter, however, appears unrelated.

[3] Possibly Anthony H. Eyre, made Lt. in 1778 (*Army List* (1786), 56). He is not listed further and may have returned to London to work in the War Office as an aide.

[4] Untraced.

[5] Admiral Sir George Bowyer (1740–1800), made Rear Admiral in 1793.

[6] The bay north of Brixham in S. Devon.

George Coleridge to Ann Bowdon Coleridge

*c.*1796–1809

Address: To Mrs Coleridge Senior, Ottery St Mary

Exeter, Monday morn, [1796–1809][1]

My dear Mother,

I know that you are anxious to hear how I am, and I have the pleasure to inform you that I amend daily. I am, to be sure, as yet a little *nash*,[2] as they call it in your country, and cannot get out into the air, but I shall attempt to do it, as soon as the weather will permit. We intend to come home the latter end of this week, or the beginning of the next, as I expect all my scholars by the end of that week.[3] I hope you made yourself very happy with your numerous friends, who daily visit you. We ought to be much obliged to them for their kindness, as you have nothing to communicate to them in return, except a few culinary maxims or so; and you know as you are not very quick in your hearing, they must take more trouble than ordinary to make you hear: but this has one advantage, as they exercise their lungs, and let the passengers in the Street partake of the entertainment.

I am made much of here. The great Drawing room is set apart for my use with a large fire in it every day and Mrs Luke Coleridge[4] is so tender to me, that no stranger has scarcely been allowed to look on my revered Person, lest I should be induced to talk or to do anything contrary to Medical advice. I know not how I shall conduct myself after all this oriental luxury in my little windy parlour and dirty school, but these changes are very right, as it teaches us to think of those who have no comforts at all, and to pity them.

---

[1] Pencil in another hand; the dating derives from George's wedding to Jane Hart in 1796 ('My wife') and the death of his mother. He obliquely refers to her as 'middle-aged'. In 1796 she was 69 and died at the age of 82.

[2] *nash*: *OED* gives slang for 'quitting or going away' but the use here implies a health condition.

[3] In 1794 George was appointed head of the King's School at Ottery, a position held by his father until his death in 1781; George retired in 1808. When he arrived, there were ' "one or two scholars . . . and the schoolroom was used for keeping rabbits and poultry" '. He greatly improved the school, overcame its dozen years of neglect, and taught close to 200 pupils (*OSM* 37, 39).

[4] Sara Hart Coleridge, widowed in 1790.

My sister Betsey[5] is here and very well. She braves all weather, even the east wind, which few of our family are hardy enough to attack. She desires to be kindly remembered to you and all at Ottery. Mrs Luke Coleridge has partly taken a servant of most extraordinary qualities, and the only difference of opinion at present, is about a white gown, which the maid has been used to wear. I recommend it to be dyed black, what think you?

If you want anything from Exeter I hope you will send word before we come home. I dare say the Milliners have got down from London some new fashionable winter Bonnets for middle-aged Ladies. I shall be happy to procure one for you, if you wish it, as I know you love to be a little fashionable.

I am very grateful to all my Ottery friends for their kind inquiries after my health, and I hope I shall have an opportunity on my return of personally waiting on them. I receive Company now, and have had today Mr Nation,[6] Mr Baledge[7] to see me.

My wife[8] (thank God) is very well and so would Mrs Luke have been had she not tumbled down over the stairs and shaken her frame almost to dissolution. She is however able to get down sufficient nourishment to keep life and soul together.

All Friends here send kindest Love and remembrance to you, and I am, my dear Mother, at all times and seasons, Your dutiful and affectionate son,

                                        George Coleridge

Mrs Brown[9] will not send George this weather.

[5] George's half-sister Elizabeth (1751–1815), who married Jacob Phillips of Exeter. *Ante* No. 7, William Coleridge to Revd John Coleridge, 1779–80.

[6] Possibly William Nation, a vicar living in Exeter. His only son William (b. 1791) attended Cambridge and was later in the Middle Temple (J. S. Venn, *Alumni Cantabrigienses 1752–1900* (Cambridge: University Press), iv. 516).

[7] Untraced.

[8] Jane (Jenny) Hart Coleridge, engaged to William Coleridge before his death in 1780, and sister of Sara Hart Coleridge.

[9] Untraced.

George Coleridge to *Ann Bowdon Coleridge*

16 JANUARY 1809

Address: To Mrs Dowager Coleridge, Ottery St Mary

Jan. 16, 1809[1]

My dear Mother,

If I had known that you had a particular wish that I should write to you I would have done it. But as it has not been my custom so to do, and as my writing is very unintelligible to you I should not have written but from your express wish. That wish is quite sufficient, as I am desirous to gratify you in every reasonable desire which you can form, and which is at all practicable. I know if you could express your wishes to me, one of the first would be, and a very natural one it is, that your Children should live in Amity and Friendship, inasmuch as no command is more express in the Gospel than the forgiving of injuries, and that too not *outwardly*, but from the bottom of the heart. Now hear me, dear Mother, and I speak to you before God as my witness, that I look on the forgiveness of injuries as absolutely necessary to secure my eternal salvation, and that therefore I make it my daily prayer to God that I may not offend in this great point. And it has pleased God of his great Mercy hitherto to keep my heart so disposed, that I have neither acted maliciously in deed, nor in word, nor I trust in thought. Secondly that with my mind in this frame I have been desirous of reconciliation wherever and whenever it could be *sincerely* effected as the best proof of my sincerity. But you must be aware that there are two parties in all such cases, and that unless both unite in a sincere desire to live in Christian peace that no good can be effected. And I must tell you plainly that in the case of my Brother Edward I have never witnessed any such desire; but that whenever we have any intercourse, the rent is always made worse.[2]

Let me next, my dear Mother, rectify a mistake into which you seem to have fallen, viz: that I have bad advisers. Now you do *me* an

---

[1] Ann Coleridge would die in November 1809.

[2] The nature of the quarrel cannot be established. STC wrote a short fragment on 'Disagreements among Friends' (British Library EG 2800, fo. 171). There are a few parallels to George's thinking in this letter. STC says third parties should not interfere 'for this is one of the very few cases, in which Procrastination is virtuous'.

injustice by supposing that I could be so weak as to ask or receive advice from any *human* being, on a subject which Christ-Jesus has so clearly explained: and you do my *Friends* an injustice by supposing them so wicked as to prolong so unnatural a separation. Be assured that I am *alone* responsible to God for my conduct in this business, and that I verily expect at his awful tribunal to give an account of every action done in the flesh. I have therefore never explained my feelings on the subject to the world, because Man is not to be my Judge, but God. 'Vengeance is mine,' says God 'I will repay'.[3] Assure yourself therefore, my dear Mother, that it is not my custom to vindicate my cause before men to catch a little ready approbation, but on the contrary it is my practice (and I speak to you as before God) to pray individually for every member of my family, and for every one with equal sincerity that God Almighty will be pleased to pour down his holy Spirit in their hearts, which, and which alone, will assuredly lead to Christian peace. All other help is as ineffectual as it is impossible. I have never yet seen the interference of friends do any good to reconciling men, unless they themselves have the Spirit of reconciliation within them, and this Spirit is from God and not from Man. Make yourself therefore, dear Mother, perfectly contented, for in God's good time all things will be reconciled.

You know I suppose that I have been under Mr Patch's[4] care for a small wound in the back of my leg ever since I came to Exeter. I am still under his care and do not go out of doors, but I am in other respects well and very contented with my situation, seeing that nothing happens without God's permission. My School[5] will open very large after the Holidays. And I hope God will give me health and spirits to fulfill my duty. The demands on my pocket are so numerous, that without some advantage from the school, I should not be able to comply with them and this would be a real grief to me. I have the satisfaction to say that Mrs Phillips[6] is considerably better and desires with Mrs Luke, my good wife, William and George[7] their

---

[3] Romans 12: 19.

[4] Robert Patch, surgeon (d. 1813), or possibly either Burnet Patch, wine merchant, apothecary, and Mayor of Exeter (d. 1815), or Philip Patch, apothecary (d. 1821).

[5] Not the King's School, since George resigned his position there in 1808. *Ante* No. 38, George Coleridge to Ann Bowdon Coleridge, 1796–1809, n. 3. He began to teach in Exeter.

[6] His half-sister Elizabeth had married Jacob Phillips of Exeter.

[7] William Hart Coleridge (1789–1849), son of Luke Herman Coleridge and Sarah Hart, and later Bishop of Barbados, and George May Coleridge (1798–1847), son of George Coleridge and Jane Hart. They were cousins, STC's nephews, and Ann Bowdon Coleridge's grandsons.

kindest love and duty to you. Accept, my dear Mother the same from
your dutiful son,

Geo: Coleridge

P.S. I will thank you to tell John at the Warden House[8] that I would
have him clear the gutters of snow before the thaw comes on.

[8] The Warden's House, near the south-western corner of St Mary's churchyard. Ann
Coleridge had moved there from the School House after the death of her husband (*OSM*
67).

No. 40

Charles Close[1] to *Francis George Coleridge*[2]

26 JANUARY 1836

Exeter, Jan. 26, 1836

My dear Sir:

I am sorry you should consider any apology necessary in applying for any information Mrs Lewis[3] could give you as to any particulars connected with your Uncles who died in India and can only regret that they are so scanty. It appears that Capt. John Coleridge is the only one here alluded to. Mrs Lewis says she recollects perfectly his coming round from Calcutta to Tillicherry for his health, that he was a very gentlemanly looking man, and that his regimentals hung upon him like a sack,[4] and she conceives by the Tenor of the letter that Mrs Lewis must have been well acquainted with him when he had been at Calcutta as she speaks of him as our Friend Coleridge. I am going to write to General Dick[5] who belonged to the Bengal Presidency and may possibly have been acquainted with one or both of your Uncles,[6] and should be able to forward me any particulars. I will lose no time in communicating them.

With kind remembrances to Mrs Coleridge, Believe me, my dear Sir, Very sincerely yours,

Chas Close

Enclosed Copy of Letter from Mrs Lewis to Capt: Archdeacon.[7]

[1] Untraced.

[2] Francis George Coleridge (1794–1854), solicitor, a younger son of James Coleridge and nephew of STC. It was he who met by chance and then entertained Wordsworth in late May 1841 when the poet visited Ottery St Mary, apparently for the only time. Making the trip rather than attend his own daughter's wedding, Wordsworth wrote, 'These were farewell visits for life and, of course, not a little interesting' (*OSM* 71, 98; *MNH*, App. C).

[3] *Ante* No. 31, Mrs Lewis to Capt. John Archdeacon, 26 Sept. 1787. This and the next two sentences are confusing. It seems Mrs Lewis is still alive, but that another 'she' is interpreting her letter.

[4] John Coleridge may have been suffering from malaria and depression.

[5] George Dick, appointed Major General in 1821 (*Army List* (1836), 55).

[6] John and Francis Syndercombe Coleridge.

[7] No. 31.

Appendix: Letter Numbers

Present Edition No.	Add. MS 47556 No.
1	2 (fos. 15–16)
2	33 (fo. 71)
3	3 (fos. 17–18)
4	20 (fos. 48–50)
5	36 (fo. 74)
6	4 (fos. 19–20)
7	28 (fos. 64–6)
8	Not numbered (fo. 13)
9	19 (fos. 46–7)
10	21 (fo. 51)
11	1 (fo. 14)
12	5 (fo. 21)
13	6 (fos. 22–22b)
14	12 (fo. 35)
15	31 (fo. 69)
16	7 (fo. 23)
17	32 (fo. 70)
18	27 (fos. 62–3)
19	13 (fos. 36, 36b, 37)
20	14 (fos. 38–38b)
21	30 (fo. 68)
22	8 (fos. 24–5)
23	9 (fo. 26)
24	10 (fos. 27–8)
25	11 (fos. 29–31)
26	15 (fos. 39–39b)
27	16 (fo. 40)
28	22 (fos. 52–3)
29	34 (fo. 73)
30	29 (fo. 67)
31	Included with No. 40 (fos. 76–7)
32	35 (fo. 72)
33	24 (fos. 56–7)
34	23 (fos. 54–5)
35	17 (fos. 41–3)
36	18 (fos. 44–5)
37	37 (fo. 75)
38	25 (fos. 58–9)
39	26 (fos. 60–1)
40	38 (fo. 76)

Index

In the following Index, published works are listed by title rather than author except for Samuel Taylor Coleridge. His published writings are listed under VII. WORKS following his entries.

Christ's Hospital 10, 12, 13, 14, 15–16,
    17, 18, 20, 60 n., 61 n., 75 n., 89 n.
Church of St Mary, *see* St Mary's Church
Clapp, John 28 n.
Clapp, Robert 28 n.
Clapp, Sarah 28 n.
Clapt, Mr, *see* Clapp, Robert
Clinton, Admiral George 47 n.
Close, Charles 104
Coburn, Kathleen 5
Coffin, Mrs 46
Coleridge, Alwyn 5
Coleridge, Ann Bowdon 6, 8, 11, 13, 15,
    16–17, 18, 27 n., 45, 56, 58, 64 n.,
    69, 93
  character of 41
  health 77
  Luke hopes she will visit London 60
  efforts to enlist STC in army 80
  receives money from Frank, 82–3, 85
  keeps Frank's gold watch, 97 n.
  moves to Warden's House 103 n.
Coleridge, Anne (Nancy) 2, 8, 11, 12, 14,
    16, 18–19, 23, 53, 55, 58, 66, 69, 70,
    72, 80, 87–8, 89–90, 91, 95–6
  works at Exeter 52, 54, 72 n.
  John reflects on her work at Exeter 74
  death of 14, 15, 22, 96 n.
Coleridge, Bernard John Seymour, 2nd
    Baron Coleridge 1, 3, 4, 5, 24–25
  further research 12, 24–25, 94, 97
Coleridge, Derwent 5
Coleridge, Edward (Ned) 23, 41, 42, 48,
    72, 93
  dispute with George 101–2
Coleridge, Elizabeth (Betsey), *see* Phillips,
    Elizabeth
Coleridge, Francis George 104
Coleridge, Francis Syndercombe (Frank)
    1, 4, 5, 6–7, 8, 9, 10, 12, 13, 15, 16,
    18, 19, 21, 53, 56, 67, 70, 75, 94
  joins navy 11
  leaves home 7, 23, 50
  army career 25, 52, 55, 58, 59, 65, 97
  nurses STC 19, 41 n.
  second father theme 49 n., 56, 78
  hopes to marry Maria Northcote 56 n.,
    92
  meets John in India 62–3
  hopes to send money home 66–7
  studies Persian 66, 68, 72
  separated from John 68, 72, 77
  helps family financially 71, 79, 82–3, 85

affection for Molly 78, 95
health 85
reports John's death 91
death of 14, 22, 93 n.; as suicide 12,
    22, 92
Coleridge, George 2, 6, 13, 14, 15, 18, 19,
    22, 34 n., 69, 72, 83, 89, 93, 102
  as second father to STC 49 n.
  effort to enlist STC in army 80
  comforts mother 87–8
  plans to return to Hackney 89
  at Newcome's School 40 n.
  helps secure STC's release from army
    98 n.
  health 99–100
  head of King's School 99 n.
  marriage to Jane Hart 46–7 n., 77 n.,
    99 n.
  dispute with Edward 101–2
  reassures mother 101–2
  resigns from King's School 99 n.
  teaches in Exeter 102 n.
Coleridge, George May 102 n.
Coleridge, James 17, 31 n., 37, 46, 54, 59,
    64 n., 70, 74, 87–8, 93, 94
  marriage to Frances Taylor 28 n., 30 n.
  military career 23, 57, 74
  receives money from John 68 n.
  writes from Dublin 71
  expects help from John 71, 75
  nominated to command a company 98
  helps secure STC's release from army
    98 n.
Coleridge, Jane (Jenny) Hart 6, 46–7 n.,
    88
  engagement to William 100 n.
  marriage to George 77 n., 99 n.
Coleridge, (Revd) John 2, 3, 4, 5, 6, 8,
    14, 15, 18, 19, 27, 33 n., 37, 38, 40,
    47 n., 72 n.
  sons as tribe of brothers 39 n.
  writings as model for STC 20
  health of 40 n., 45
  translates *Phormio* 42 n.
  arranges for Frank to join navy 50
  accompanies Frank to Plymouth 51
  visits Hart family 77 n.
  death of 6, 14, 22, 40 n., 47 n., 49 n.,
    50 n.
Coleridge, John 4, 5, 6, 10, 11, 12, 13, 16,
    17, 18, 19, 22, 23, 27, 32, 54
  service in India 23, 25, 38, 58, 59, 65
  military records 25, 94